PRAISE FOR *HISTORIC HENDERSON COUNTY: TALES FROM ALONG THE RIDGES*

"What a wonderful discovery of additional works by Louise Bailey, a true Southern lady with a sophisticated, down-to-earth way of telling real mountain stories. I'm glad our paths in life crossed, if only for brief periods of time."
—Arthur Cooley, president, WHKP Radio, Hendersonville

"I thought there would be no more stories from the richness of Louise Bailey's memories, yet here is a new collection of essays that Louise had intended to publish as a book. The words and images of Henderson County's 'olden days' that come from her pen are invaluable to those of us who know that the present has been built on the past. My thanks to Joe Jr. and Terry."
—Ann B. Ross, author of the Miss Julia novels

"We mountainfolk have pride and we don't like to be preached to or talked down to. Louise Bailey does neither. She speaks as one of us, proud to be who she is and genuinely respectful of those who approach life with courage and a spirit of 'get up and go.' She reveals in her publications the heart of our people, and, in so doing, she celebrates this place we call home."
—Tom E. Orr, playwright and retired Hendersonville High School drama teacher

"Once again Louise Bailey has blessed us with her recollections of life here in these beautiful mountains that many of us have called home for years. And she has blessed those that did not grow up here with her memories through her words. Thank you again, Louise."
—Jeff Miller, Henderson County business owner and HonorAir founder, senatorial candidate

"A historian's primary charge is to be an accurate chronicler of facts. Good historians additionally provide a solid sense of time and place. The best in the field weave a colorful narrative, acquainting the reader with people amidst their life experiences. Louise Howe Bailey accomplished all three objectives in her columns and books. What good news that readers may once again hear from her in these remembrances."
—Mary Garrison, *Hendersonville Times-News* columnist and author

HISTORIC HENDERSON COUNTY

Tales from Along the Ridges

LOUISE HOWE BAILEY

FOREWORD BY ROBERT MORGAN,
COMPILED BY TERRY RUSCIN & JOSEPH BAILEY JR.

THE History PRESS

Published by The History Press
Charleston, SC 29403
www.historypress.net

Front cover, top: Oxen hauling logs in Pisgah Forest, early 1900s. *Photo courtesy of John Paul Jones. Bottom*: Site of Rhett's Mill and the Old Mill Playhouse. *Photo by Terry Ruscin. Back cover, left*: A moonshiner tends his still. *Photo courtesy of the Henderson County Genealogical and Historical Society Inc. Right*: 1800s log cabin on Teneriffe property in Flat Rock. *Photo by Terry Ruscin with permission of Helen and Marvin Seibold.*

First published 2010

Manufactured in the United States

ISBN 978.1.60949.102.4

Library of Congress Cataloging-in-Publication Data

Bailey, Louise Howe.
Historic Henderson County : tales from along the ridges / Louise Howe Bailey ; compiled by Terry Ruscin and Joe Bailey ; foreword by Robert Morgan.
p. cm.
Includes index.
ISBN 978-1-60949-102-4
1. Henderson County (N.C.)--History--Anecdotes. 2. Henderson County (N.C.)--Social life and customs--Anecdotes. I. Ruscin, Terry, 1951- II. Bailey, Joe, 1948- III. Title.
F262.H47B358 2010
975.6'92--dc22
2010040433

Also by Louise Howe Bailey

Along the Ridges
Go Home Wi' Me
Draw Up a Chair
From Rock Hill to Connemara: The Story Before Carl Sandburg
50 Years with the Vagabonds
St. John in the Wilderness, 1836–
Generations of Excellence: A History of Pardee Hospital
Remembering Henderson County: A Legacy of Lore
Remembering Henderson County: A Legacy of Lore—Memorial Edition

Coauthor of
Hendersonville and Henderson County: A Pictorial History

Dedicated to the memory of Fanny, Mary, Ellen and "Bub" Stepp, and all the other courageous and honorable pioneers of Henderson County, North Carolina.

Contents

CONTENTS

Foreword

It is a particular pleasure to have this further volume of essays from Louise Howe Bailey. During her long life, she gave so much to the community, to the region and to the reading public. And now we have yet another collection of informative, inspiring and entertaining articles. She is still blessing us with her wisdom and extraordinary knowledge of local history. She was a special friend to me and to many others in Henderson County and beyond.

The first literary event I ever participated in—in Henderson County—was a meet-the-author luncheon organized by Opportunity House in the summer of 1970. Louise Bailey arranged for me to be one of the speakers at that luncheon, held one Sunday at Clifton's Cafeteria.

Before I knew Louise Bailey, I knew her husband, Dr. Joseph Bailey, who was our family physician. It was Dr. Bailey who treated my childhood illnesses and conducted the physicals for my admission to college and to obtain a marriage license. He was the physician for my son's birth, and he treated my wife's asthma. I first met Louise Bailey when I was helping my dad paint Argyle, the Judge Mitchell King summer home in Flat Rock. Louise and her husband were making a call on Mr. and Mrs. Alec King, who owned the historic house. I had read Louise's column in the *Hendersonville Times-News* and knew she was descended from Judge King. We talked that day about local history and writing, and we remained friends ever after.

One of the most important genres of writing and scholarship is local history. It is the local historian who gathers and communicates the intimate details, the fine print and the oral traditions of a region's past. The local historian is a crucial link between oral history, folk narrative and preservation of a written record in public media. Future writers and other writers of history rely on the local historian to preserve and bring alive on the page the people, the places, the voices, the pictures, the humor, the sacrifices and the heroes of everyday life. Without local historians we would be blind to much that has happened, to much of who we are, where we have been and where we are going. The local historian gives us a living sense of our community across time. No one makes us feel as connected to a place and to a people.

I can think of no finer example of a local historian than Louise Bailey. Henderson County has been extremely blessed to have her in our midst to tell our stories, to us and to the world at large. For over forty years, she instructed and entertained us with accounts of our past, often letting folks tell their own stories. She was as interested in the people of the hollows and back ridges as those in the grand mansions of Flat Rock. No one has ever known as much about the region or made so many friends in Henderson County as Louise Bailey. She devoted much of her life to listening, observing, recording and reporting the lives around her, the legends, the landscapes, the storms and tragedies, the humanity of our people.

Louise Howe Bailey was born in Henderson County, the daughter of Dr. William Bell White Howe, a beloved physician who served both the Flat Rock community and the mountain people. Dr. Howe made his daily calls around the county, traveling muddy roads and trails on horseback, by buggy, on a motorcycle and, later, by motorcar. As a girl, Louise accompanied her father on his rounds and made friends with scores of county people. Little did she guess that even then she was preparing herself to become their spokesperson, their historian.

Louise was educated at Fassifern School, and she, when young, was something of a tomboy, preferring camping expeditions in the wilderness to tea dances and fashion shows. She graduated from Winthrop College, taught high school English for two years and studied library science at Columbia University in New York. But she always returned to Henderson County and kept her contacts with both the people and the place.

When she returned to Flat Rock as a young woman, Louise got to know the Sandburg family and served the poet and biographer as an assistant, typing the epic novel *Remembrance Rock*. But it was the local people who inspired Louise in her life's work.

"I realize the privilege it has been for me," Louise has written, "to associate with many people who followed a lifestyle much like that of their forebears. While some of them spent their lives far beyond the beaten paths, they were nevertheless a significant part of our history that needs to be recorded before it is lost in the rush of progress."

To explain how she began writing local history, Louise said:

> *In the late 1960s I talked to a couple of small groups about my association with the mountain people. The editor of our newspaper at that time heard about it and asked me to submit a few short articles for him to consider printing on a weekly basis. I was ecstatic. I felt the information I had was an important aspect of local history. Yet I knew that privacy meant everything to the people about whom I would be writing.*

Note both the enthusiasm and sensitivity to the nature of her subjects.

In her writing over the years, Louise Bailey gave us local lives and voices, living voices. She told us of the blind harmonica player Elzie Floyd and of the colony of freed slaves called the Kingdom of the Happy Land. She told us ghost stories and recounted the life of Christopher Memminger, secretary of the treasury for the Confederacy. She wrote about the old courthouse and the founding of Hendersonville. She served as our chronicler and as the *memory* of the community.

It is especially important at this moment in our history, when Henderson County is changing rapidly—with the swelling influx of retirees from the Northeast and from Florida, year-round tourists, a growing Hispanic community, new businesses and industries, new educators and new talent, new building and new leadership—to remember, record and recount our past, to know who we were and where we have been. Such knowledge will enable us to meet the new challenges with greater confidence, for in some ways the present is already a foreign country, and we must move forward intelligently and responsibly. No one has taught us more about our heritage than Louise Bailey. She has served as our essential guide to the past, reminding us of our achievements with humor and respect. She has reminded us of who we are, and what she has told us is what we will pass on to our children and future generations.

—Robert Morgan

Preface

During my mother's last two or three years of life, she often mentioned to me that she would like to publish another book—a collection of some of the stories she had written for the local newspaper, the *Hendersonville Times-News*, over the past ten years or so. Unfortunately, she never managed to find the time to get the book organized and off to a publisher.

Recognizing the legacy of the histories and lifestyles that she so skillfully recorded with her vivid descriptions and her sharp sense of humor, I wanted to do something to continue the preservation of these memories for the benefit of not only the descendants of the very people about whom she wrote, but also for the new residents of Henderson County. What better way to do that than to see such a book become a reality?

Having never before published a book, I was very much at a loss about how to go about it. Although I had copies of all of Mother's stories from the time in question, I certainly had no idea what to do next. A quick conversation, however, with Mother's good friend and author himself Terry Ruscin assured me that I had contacted just the right person. When I asked him if he would mind providing me with a little guidance and direction, it was obvious that he would enjoy nothing more. Virtually all I needed to do was supply Terry with the stories, and he would do the rest—to my great relief! It is through Terry's efforts that you are holding this book in your hands today. I am and shall be eternally grateful for his efforts, and I know that Mother would be most happy with the outcome.

Mother's constant goal in writing about Henderson County was to record and preserve the memories of the people who were our pioneers and forebears, to describe how these people survived in a time without the conveniences we all now take for granted and to take you, the reader, along as a travel companion on many of the forays she made herself along the ridges and into the homes of some of her subjects.

Read how mountain men extracted heavy timber from steep mountainsides without the aid of machinery. And did you know that Hendersonville was once known as "the 'dancingest' town in America"? Visit and meet the Stepp family and learn how they coped without any of the conveniences we call indispensible today. Find out why Flat Rock was known as "the little Charleston of the mountains." Where was the Kingdom of the Happy Land? What kinds of stores and shops were popular on Hendersonville's Main Street long ago? Did you know that physicians regularly made house calls, even if it required them to walk part of the way? And where would you guess was a favorite place to drop off illegal mountain moonshine?

Not many of us can claim to have a really valuable and meaningful legacy to pass on to future generations. Mother certainly did. I hope that through this book she will live on for all who knew her as she shares history and her dearest memories of the places and people that gave her life such meaning.

—Joseph Bailey Jr.

Acknowledgements

We wish to express our gratitude to the many people who assisted with reading, fact checking and supplying photographic components for this work: Virginia Thompson, Margaret Payne and Sandra Heatherly of the Henderson County Genealogical and Historical Society; C.E. ("Gene") and Debby Staton; Sandra DeVonish; Julianne Heggoy; John Paul Jones; Ashley Tate of the Carl Sandburg Home National Historic Site; Helen and Marvin Seibold of Teneriffe and Sandi and Dang Jalernpan of the Flat Rock Inn (Five Oaks), for granting permissions to photograph their properties; Enrique ("Ricky") Moreno, for lending his special touch to the contemporary photographic images; and Tabitha Brockus and the facilities of Blue Ridge Community College, for the scanning of images. We also thank Robert Morgan for writing the foreword, Jessica Berzon of The History Press for accepting and guiding this worthy project and Jaime Muel of The History Press for lending her editorial skill to the manuscript.

A Bit of Background

Watching the Seasons Change

The other morning I had no reason to hurry out of bed, so I reached for the percolator that had my cup of coffee ready and waiting for me. Settling back down, I thought how nice it was to be able to watch the seasons change right outside the windows in front of me.

I could see more than that. There's a full view of a nesting box intended to lure bluebirds, but it has been there for several years now, and it does provide living quarters, but always for wrens. Bluebirds ignore it. As industrious as the wrens are, though, they are fun to watch, and with a new year getting underway, March isn't far ahead, and that's when a pair of wrens will be moving into the box. Their *chirpety-chirps* will fill the air, welcoming the earliest—and most unpredictable—month of spring.

I couldn't just lie there, though, and think about things like that. I needed to be up and about. And it was time to get another column ready for the newspaper—but a column about what? Not a single thought came to mind. But a recollection did, popping up as recollections have a way of doing, and being different from thoughts in that they come without effort. I remembered that, a number of years ago, I had given a talk on local history to a small group in town. Mead Parce, then editor of the *Hendersonville Times-News*, heard about it and asked me to put the information into several short columns for him to judge whether they were appropriate for newspaper articles he could publish under the title "Along the Ridges." After I'd supplied a column a week for seventeen weeks, I had heard nothing more from Editor Parce, and I was about to run into trouble. I was obliged to go into his office to confess, "I'm completely out of material." He didn't even look up. "No you're not," he said, going right on with what he was doing and making it obvious that he had no time to fritter away on conversation. I went home and looked seriously into Henderson County's history. And I began to work it into columns.

I've tried to avoid repetition in the columns and am glad I usually could, because over at Blue Ridge Community College there's a little room housing bound volumes containing copies of those columns. Subject matter unavoidably recurs from time to time, but it can, and needs to be, presented from different angles. Certain individuals featured in some of the columns have advisedly remained nameless or have gone by an alias for the protection of my scalp when read by those individuals.

After forty-two years, three editors and 2,184 columns, I've taken only two weeks off from "Along the Ridges." That was when my husband was ill in the mid-1980s. I confess that writing the column has been something I've felt privileged to do, and I don't ever want to *not* do it for any length of time. Meanwhile, I'll try to find out what kind of plant is growing by the steps leading in and out of the Flat Rock Post Office. I do know from years past that it's among the first to "put out" in early spring, and give or take a few delays due to snows and ice storms, I'll be watching it to see when its buds begin to swell. I'll mark the date on my calendar, hoping that will make spring seem to get to us a little faster.

On Having a Sense of Humor

Warped as it may be, I am ever grateful for my sense of humor. Whether I inherited it or it just rubbed off on me while I was growing up, I can't say, but I do know that in either case my father had more to do with it than anyone else would have dared. He never missed an opportunity to test it, but the most drastic measure he ever took to do so happened one morning when I chose to go back to sleep instead of getting up for breakfast.

I had a downstairs bedroom at that time. Into it came my dad, dropping kernels of corn to lure our dozen white ducks onto the front porch, across the living room that was adjacent to mine and right on to my bedside. Bedlam is too mild a word to waste on what followed, but from that time on I forewent any extra shut-eye.

One morning, for some reason I've since forgotten, I was occupying an upstairs room. The sun had risen high enough to flood the room with light, yet there seemed to be a gentle, misty rain falling on my face. Rain? With the sun shining? My dad was on the ground below, aiming the garden hose through the open window beside my bed.

I must admit that ordinarily he was very proper at the dinner table and expected his children to follow his example. But there were times our devoted great-great-aunt Agnes came for her turn of two weeks in the mountains to escape the oppressive summertime heat and humidity of Charleston before air conditioning was even thought of. Charleston dinners, whatever the season, began with hot soup, and the custom continued in Flat Rock, where whoever hosted their Charleston relatives served them the popular okra soup.

My dad was brought up on it, and it remained his lifetime favorite, but not mine. The soup itself was good, though, and I got by with leaving a conspicuous glob of okra in my bowl. And I minded my manners by taking in the soup in commendable silence, but when Aunt Agnes came to visit, things were different. She audibly sipped from her spoonful. My dad did a

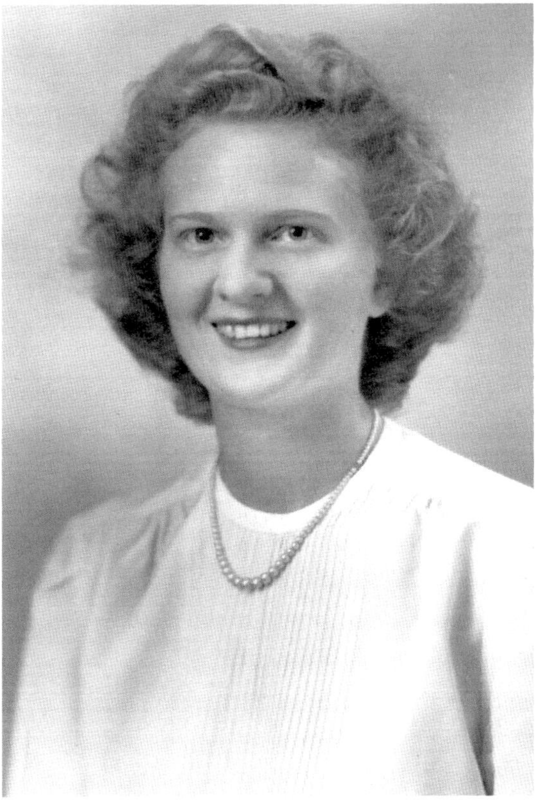

Louise Howe in her early twenties. *Photo courtesy of Joseph Bailey Jr.*

subtle imitation of it while cutting his eyes around at me until I was obliged to keep dropping my napkin in order to lean over and pick it up without Aunt Agnes seeing my laughter threatening to escape—and audibly.

Probably the time I was most grateful for a sense of humor was when my husband, Joe, and I took our twenty-two-foot cabin cruiser to the Santee-Cooper Lake in South Carolina to spend a couple of days fishing. Joe launched the boat and then brought it close enough to shore for me to wade out and climb on the back deck. We'd stopped to see some relatives on the way, so I was still in my lavender pique dress, but by lifting the skirt to my knees I would have no trouble getting out to the boat and onto it. I reached the boat and caught hold of it. It scooted forward, and I in my lavender pique dress went under.

I shot right up, and I couldn't help noticing Flippo and Stringbean, who ran the marina, trying their best to keep from laughing. As were some men standing on the dock—men from Hendersonville. They didn't even need a sense of humor to see it was a laughing matter.

I was mighty glad I had one, though, and that another attempt to board was successful.

My Father's Wisdom

Don't Judge a Person by His or Her Appearance

My father—Dr. William B.W. Howe III, or "Old Doc" as many knew him—used to tell me not to judge a person by his or her appearance. In spite of his advice, I continue to remember a particular individual who observed the current styles, matched his colors and, whatever the occasion, seemed appropriately dressed for it. Retired from what was undoubtedly a lucrative position and having no family to support, he was able to portray quality on whatever occasion it was called for. At the same time, he had an uncommonly practical outlook that directed him through situations in a manner somewhat different from the usual.

There was the time he bought a pair of trousers that needed to be shortened an inch or so in length. He declined the salesman's offer to make the adjustment for whatever the cost was at that time. He said he could do it himself, and that was what he did, but without a needle and thread. He did it with staples. He made sure the little wire pieces were hidden by the weave of the material, although he didn't suppose anyone could possibly see them way down at his ankles.

As I said, the man had a practical streak. For example, he was known to have a lifetime supply of unused wallets stashed away in a dresser drawer. For years, friends and relatives had given him wallets at Christmastime, hoping he would be inspired to throw away the old one that was not only noticeably scarred but also was held shut by a dingy strip of duct tape. People in his company reached for their neat leather billfolds that gaped open at the slightest touch. He peeled back the dingy strip of duct tape that held his wallet shut, and then he methodically counted out what he needed to make the payment he owed.

We can only imagine the concern—more likely the distress—of that frugal man when he realized time had taken its toll on his old automobile and he would be obliged to give it up for a new one. He hated to drive anyway, but transportation was essential, and he had no choice but to go to a dealership and make a selection. You know how he must have dreaded looking at all the available cars and hearing the accolades paid each one by the salesman, but when he had done it for as long as he thought necessary, to his great relief he settled himself in a chair in the manager's office and waited patiently while the dealer brought out a sheaf of papers and explained the plan for payments—and interest—over a period of time. The dealer showed him where to ink his name on the papers.

The man took his wallet from his pocket. He propped his elbows on the desk and began peeling back the dingy duct tape. The dealer watched, and then, with no explanation whatsoever, he lopped $100 off the price of the car. The customer thanked him and continued peeling bills from the roll he had taken out of his wallet until the entire cost of the car lay on the desk. No interest was included. He didn't owe any. What he would have spent on interest if he were buying on time remained in the antiquated wallet with the duct tape snugly sealing it in.

I know my dad would have called my attention to the man's good business deal in saving up the money before buying the car instead of doing it the other way around. He would have reminded me, too, that the shiny new car presented a different picture in general, but the man was still the same. He went on stapling his trouser legs to make them the right length.

DON'T BE A RUBBER STAMP

"Don't be a rubber stamp. Be yourself." My dad said it to me every time peer pressure threatened to rattle parental authority. "But everybody is doing it" fell on deaf ears, and as a result I spent more time on family camping trips in the Okefenokee Swamp than on the dance floor. I hiked up Pinnacle, Pisgah and Glassy Mountains instead of taking piano lessons. And I look back on experiences I feel ever so fortunate to have had—except the one when a cottonmouth moccasin hung from a bush beside the Okefenokee Canal. As we poled past it, my dad said, "If it drops into the boat you'll have to jump out"—into the canal with the alligators and yard-wide biting turtles. And

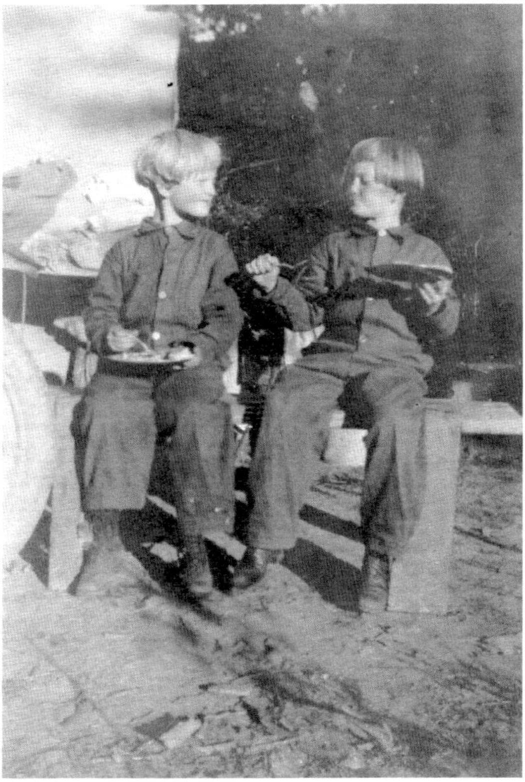

Right: Louise (left) and Jennie (right) on a camping trip. *Photo courtesy of Joseph Bailey Jr.*

Below: The Howe family camping on the Okefenokee Swamp. *Photo courtesy of Joseph Bailey Jr.*

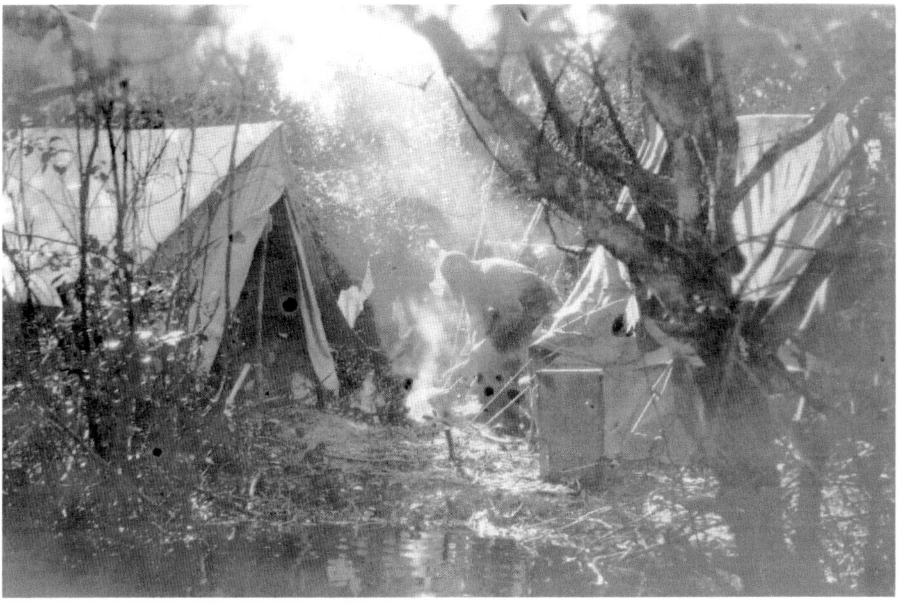

the alligator sunning on the bank just then silently slipped into the water and swam underneath our boat on his way to the opposite side.

Daddies don't bring up daughters the way mamas do. Ours was in charge of my sister, Jennie, and me from the time she was five years old and I was three. He was a young doctor building up a practice that reached across Henderson County, from mountaintops into valleys, at all hours of the day and night. We were living with our grandmother, but her health was failing, and there had to be someone to look after us. Our dad went up on Pinnacle Mountain and hired sixty-two-year-old Mary Stepp to leave her pioneer lifestyle and move in with us. From the moment her brother, "Bub," turned his mule team and wagon into our yard to deliver her to our house, she was with Jennie and me day and night until seven years later, when our dad married a schoolteacher to whom Jennie and I introduced him.

During those seven years, one or another of Mary's nieces cooked for us, but Mary ran the house, milked the cow and fed the chickens. She planted a vegetable garden and flower beds, and many afternoons she scrubbed us with Octagon Soap—the big brown bar with the coupon on the wrapper—and put us in "nice" dresses to walk the mile into town to visit with acquaintances along the sidewalks.

I often think of Mary's first day on the job.

She had sat briefly in the living room talking with our grandmother while Jennie and I watched her shyly. After awhile, she said to us, "Come on. Let's go into the woods and build you 'uns a playhouse."

Later that day, she went into the kitchen at the far end of the back porch. Jennie and I were playing in our room at the other end of the porch. A plate glass door opened into our room. Jennie stuffed some loose papers into the trash burner that kept us warm before a furnace was installed. Flames flared, prompting a lusty yell from Jennie, who thought the stove was on fire. It wasn't, but Mary wasted no time getting to it and dowsing the fire. When our dad came home that evening, we watched him put stitches into Mary's chin and forehead while she apologized for the damage she had done to the door. "Doctor," she said, "I ain't use to all that glass, and I jist didn't see it." There were no inside doors in her house on Pinnacle Mountain.

During the years she was with us, Mary took Jennie and me to spend a few days with her sister, Ellen, and brother, Bub, when they needed her to help plant or harvest crops, rob bees and hunt baby lambs on the mountainside—before wolves finally did away with them altogether. The house had two rooms downstairs, two upstairs, but no conveniences at all. Water was brought up a steep hill from a spur of Dismal Creek.

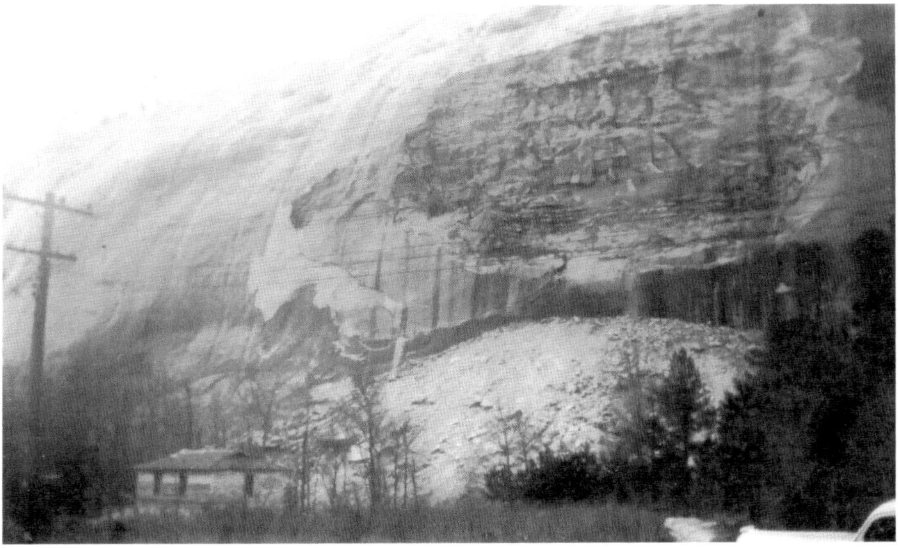

The sheer granite face of Whiteside Mountain. *Photo courtesy of Joseph Bailey Jr.*

Memories of visits on Pinnacle include everyday dinners of home-cured ham, chicken, homegrown vegetables and both corn pone and biscuits. Memories are of Ellen carding wool and spinning yarn to knit winter sweaters. And there are special memories of camping trips on Whiteside Mountain in December, when hunting was good and some of Mary's kin drove the sixty miles there in a mule-drawn wagon to camp with us and to cook mountain boomers (a kind of squirrel) for us over an open fire. Ours were never ready-made campsites. They were clearings made with axe and hatchet and at times were framed by icicles hanging from rock ledges above our tents.

Around the campfire at night I heard stories told by grandchildren and great-grands of those stalwart, self-reliant people who had come as pioneer settlers to the Western North Carolina mountains. As I grew up, I jotted down many of those stories, for they portrayed the lives of people who had carved a homeland within a mountain wilderness. Through them, unexpected opportunities have come my way, affording me opportunities I would never have had otherwise and enriching the memories that keep me company as time goes by. I can still see Mary, who was always on camping trips with us, dragging fallen limbs from woods to firesides. I remember well the time our car was mortally stuck in red clay ruts, and Mary, with the strength of a man, ripped a plank from an abandoned bridge to help lift a wheel from the mud.

I don't recall ever hearing Mary raise her voice to steer Jennie and me out of trouble, nor being upset with us when we got into it anyway. We loved her dearly, and I look back now on the privilege it was to have been in her care.

The Backbone of Summer Is Broken

I can hear my father now. "The backbone of summer is broken," he always announced in mid-July when he heard katydids begin their annual stridulating. Books tell us the male katydids make all the noise with "transparent drum-like structures at the base of their wings where the outer covers have rasps and ridges, the friction of which, when one rubs against the other as the wings are raised and lowered," produces the familiar call we hear on late summer and early autumn evenings. The call is received by other katydids through a particular place of hearing on the upper part of the front legs.

Scientists tell us the loud, shrill call of the male katydid can be heard distinctly for a quarter of a mile. While we who are accustomed to hearing it right outside our windows pay little attention to it when we're ready to go to sleep, visitors, especially children from urban areas, often find the loud and constant sound disturbing. The females are quieter, responding to the males only with chirps, but with enough of them to keep the males communicating with apparent enthusiasm until the night is half over.

Dusk used to bring bullbats flying through the yard, ridding the premises of hundreds of varieties of insects and, a number of years ago, serving as objects for riflemen practicing their marksmanship. But bullbats are not bats at all. They're birds—nighthawks—and hundreds of varieties of insects, including the anopheles mosquito that transmitted malaria, have been proven to be food for them. Potato and cucumber beetles, boll weevils and various other pests have been food for the nighthawks, so it was never smart to kill them.

The nighthawks—or bullbats, as we have known them locally—were a familiar part of our summer scene, but they're seldom seen now. Back in the days of open automobiles, though, they occasionally flew in, as one did on an occasion when my father was driving the car and an elderly passenger was on the front seat beside him. As we rounded a curve just this side of Saluda, a bullbat flew into the open car and landed against the face of the passenger, who announced with utter conviction, "Oh God, Doctor, I've swallowed a bat!"

Fortunately, she hadn't quite done that, and she was able to grab the bullbat and toss it well away from the car.

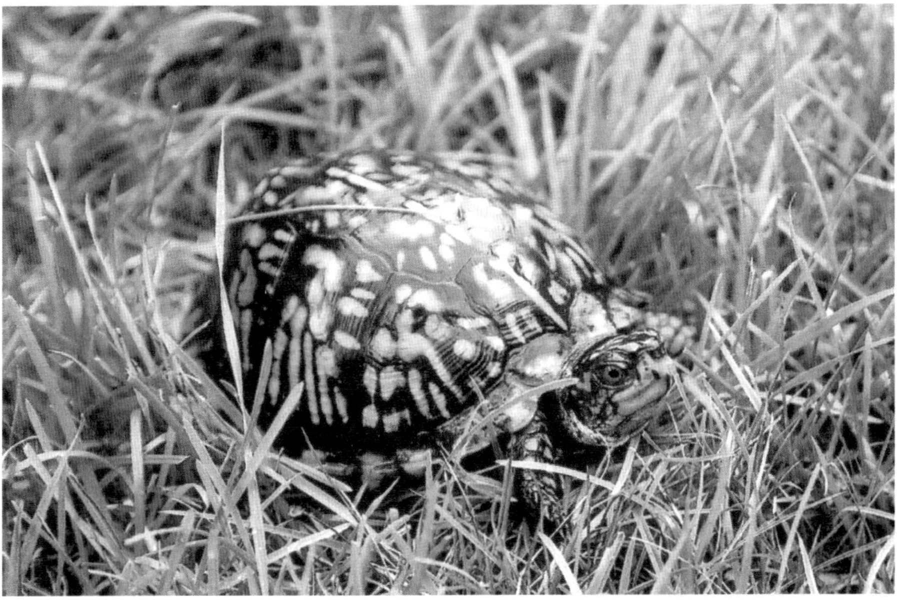

Box turtle. *Photo by Terry Ruscin.*

It's remarkable how the four-legged visitors change over the years, and we don't always know how it comes about. How, for example, and why did the coyotes find us when their natural habitat has been such a long way from here?

How have the bears become so bold—or so friendly—that they help themselves to the seeds in bird feeders hanging on patios? Personally, I still prefer the box turtles I find crossing my driveway, and I don't mind at all stopping the car, getting out and carrying a turtle out of the road. Then there's a good enough supply of baby rabbits for one or more to be sitting in the tire track as though trying to make up its mind which side of the road is the better escape route.

Summer will be over too soon, though. After all, it's mid-July now, so the backbone of it is already broken.

Kinfolk and Connections

Common Ancestors

Some people put kinfolk and "connections" in the same category, which they shouldn't do at all. We're born into our world of kinfolk and, like 'em or not, they're ours. In some cases we do a lot of boasting about certain ones who came along before us, although we personally may have gotten little more than a drop of blood from that great-great-whomever we have revered across the generations. At the same time, we say as little as possible about certain other relatives who seem to be remembered only vaguely in the dim past and are spoken of in somewhat muted tones, perhaps with a snicker now and then, by acquaintances who entertain listeners with less than complimentary recollections. What kinfolks are really supposed to do is keep in touch with one another, but some of them are negligent, while others make the most of opportunities resulting from the relationship.

"Connections" pose no real obligation for us to contact one another under ordinary circumstances, but when some do it anyway, we consider them downright thoughtful, like I did when half a dozen men and women I'd never seen nor heard of drove into my yard. Two young men stepped from the car and onto my porch. One of them handed me an envelope that had been opened, and I noticed right off that, according to the address, the letter had been forwarded. No, the young men were not soliciting. The letter was addressed to someone who used to visit us in Flat Rock in the summers when I was in my teens. It had been sent "in care of Dr. W.B.W. Howe," who, of course, was my father. For all those years, that letter had been in an old house that was at the time being done over.

The ladies got out of the car, and I ushered the whole crowd of strangers into my living room. Introductions were made and names were promptly forgotten, except that of William, who had handed me the letter. Then William began to explain who he was.

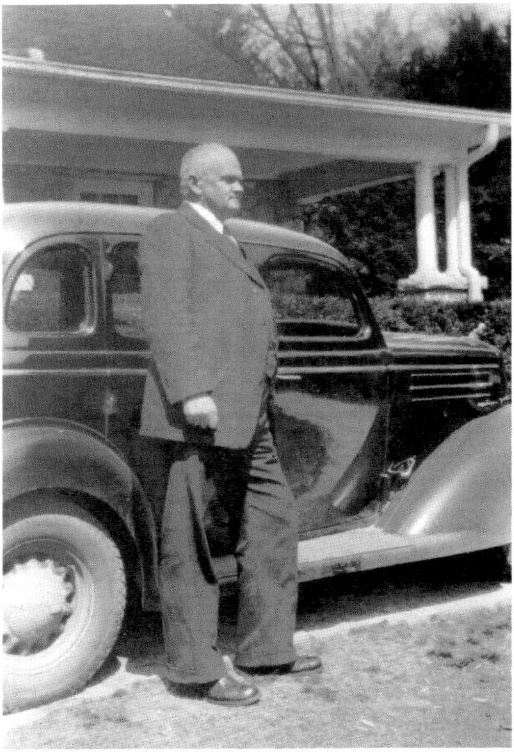

Louise Bailey's father, Dr. William Bell White Howe III ("Old Doc"), at his Flat Rock home, Laurelhurst. *Photo courtesy of Joseph Bailey Jr.*

He said his family had lived in the Virginia Shenandoah area when his grandmother was a little girl living with *her* grandmother—who was my cousin. As a college student, I had made summertime visits to that particular cousin and I had played with the little girl many times. The young man and I could in no way claim kinship, but we were definitely "connected."

I was curious to know how he had heard of me. One of the ladies in his party answered for him, saying she lives near Aiken, South Carolina. And their whole group had been at her house the previous evening. A neighbor of hers stopped in and heard their plans for a trip to the mountains. The neighbor asked if they would be going through Flat Rock, and if they were, she would like for them to give me a call. When asked how she, way down in South Carolina, happened to know someone in Flat Rock, she said, "Oh, we're 'connections.'" I was wishing I could claim her as one of my bona fide kinfolk, but she was married to one of my husband's first cousins, so I could claim her only as a "connection."

Kinfolk have the advantage—or disadvantage—of a common ancestor way back in time. Nothing can be done about that except our effort to live up to, or live down, particular traits passed on down. Connections, though, are more a matter of choice. The rest is up to us.

James King and the Family Tree

What did I tell you? April the fifteenth. Cloudy with the threat of a thunderstorm, the forecasters warned us. But there he was—a hummingbird. He wasn't poised within reach of the hole the sugar water comes out of; he was perched on the rim of the feeder, and he was going after that liquid so eagerly I wondered how far he'd come before he'd got to it. At least he hadn't let me down. According to the memo I'd jotted on my calendar, he was right on time—April the fifteenth. That was when I'd seen the first one in previous years. Now I can look where I'm going when I walk through the house instead of bumping into furniture while I watch for the first visitor of the season to pause at my hummingbird feeder.

Another pleasant surprise came on that same day in April. I found a letter from James King in my post office box. I always enjoy letters from James because they take me back many years. I know he isn't one of my kinfolk since his family name of King never had an "o" on the end of it like the Kings in my family did before my great-great-grandfather Mitchell dropped the "o" for simplicity's sake. James and I are contemporaries, though, and we played together way back when we were children. When he was ready to take his place in the business world, he moved to Michigan to work, and we lost touch with each other for many years. Now and then he returned home to the Crab Creek community where he had grown up, but I didn't know it until that day he showed up at my house.

"I'm not going to tell you who I am," he began, laughing. "You don't need to," I answered, although I hadn't seen him since we were barely out of our teens, and the thought flashed through my mind that if we can keep in touch for a few—a very few—more years, we can swap congratulations on our 100th birthdays!

In the letter I had from James, he told me he had been working on a family tree. In some ways, it must have been an easier project than his previous one, which had resulted in pieces of intricately hand-carved furniture he had given his daughters. As for the family tree, apparently he has done a thorough job of putting forebears in their rightful places, for he told me that getting the tree on paper required nine two- by three-foot sheets. Research has enabled him to include eleven generations, beginning with the first one of his King family having come from England to Jamestown and including later members who accepted land granted them in return for services rendered during the Civil War.

What a priceless county history could result if young folks today would jot down what their grandparents and, in many cases, great-grandparents can tell them. They may not find it interesting to them right now, but think how often you hear: "I wish I'd listened more carefully, but it seemed so boring back then."

James King has a big job in store for him, what with Kings and Stepps and McCalls on his family tree. He knows that a long time ago, two McCalls who must have been related married two sisters, and all of Henderson County's McCalls, as well as most of those in Transylvania County, are their descendants.

With that, he's off to a good beginning. As for the hummingbirds, I don't know just when they'll get all the way to Michigan, but James will be busy enough in the meantime.

King Reunion

Few events are more satisfying than a springtime trip to the "Holy City," as Charleston is sometimes called. Even more meaningful for me on a particular visit there was the fact that I was on my way to a King family reunion. Cousin John King, a third cousin once removed, whom I met briefly a year ago, insisted it was no trouble at all to drive from his home in Atlanta, swing by mine in Flat Rock and get right onto I-26.

I was in the backseat. A front-seat passenger's head blocked my view of turns, so I had no idea how we managed to be hurtling down Highway 11, a beautiful drive, and one of considerable length, but not heading in the direction of Charleston until a sign eventually set us straight.

Martha, the cousin who put the family gathering together, had rented a house on the Isle of Palms, where I had been many times, but never over the new bridge across the Cooper River. What a bridge that is! John was on his cellphone with Martha a number of times, being directed and redirected to where our lodging was, whether on the main highway or on a spur leading from it. But we thought of getting lost as an opportunity to see as much as possible of the island. Then Martha told us via cellphone that we were near our cottage, and we would see her standing in the yard if we turned onto the street she specified. Of course, I couldn't see through the head in front of me, but before long we were turning into a driveway, and I knew we must have arrived at the correct destination.

I was really impressed with the way my cousin John King made his way through traffic patterns I'm thankful to say Little River Road has not yet had to resort to. And our cousin Mitchell King—the only namesake of the

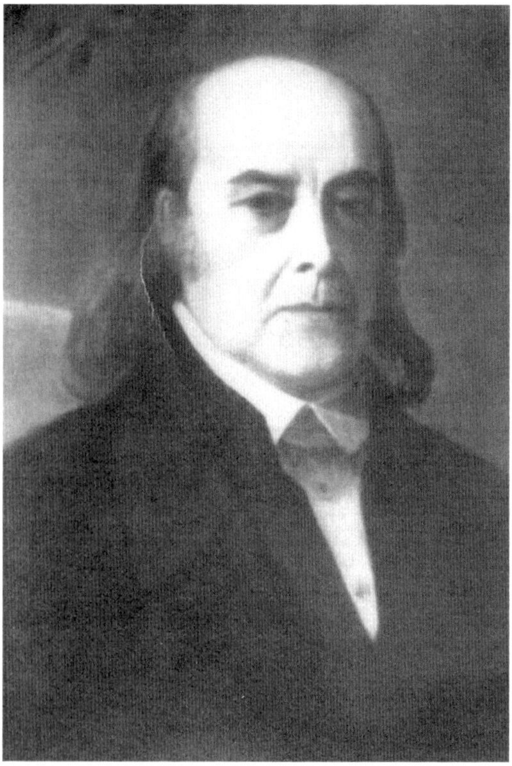

Judge Mitchell King, Louise Bailey's great-great-grandfather. *Photo courtesy of Joseph Bailey Jr.*

forebear of the assembled Kings, Judge Mitchell King, who donated fifty acres for the site of the town of Hendersonville—came from Hilton Head, wheelchair and all, to join us for lunch in Charleston. I hadn't seen Mitchell since we were in high school. At one time, his dad owned Crail Farm—now Crooked Creek—in Flat Rock. When World War II came on and rationed gasoline prevented his driving up from Atlanta, the property was sold to the Warner brothers, who brought some of their Hollywood stars there for vacations.

John King and I visited the graves of relatives in the Scots Presbyterian Churchyard, and on the way out of town Sunday we paid respects at other family graves in Magnolia Cemetery. We noted the grave of one relative several generations back whose wife and children were not beside him, although the 1850 census lists them.

Back home again I stood on my porch to wave goodbye to John King as he headed back to Atlanta. He was barely out of sight when my phone rang, and I went inside to answer it.

"This is your cousin John King. Sally and I are spending the night here on our way from Florida back to Michigan. Could you join us for breakfast?" Indeed I could. He has papers indicating his descent from the King whose wife, for whatever reason, is not with him in Magnolia Cemetery.

That John King and his cousin who gave me a ride to the family reunion had never heard of each other. But plans were already underway for a King reunion the following summer—"at your place," I was told.

Henderson County Past and Present

Kanuga Lake Colony

It's engaging to read predictions quoted in the *French Broad Hustler*, our newspaper published one hundred years ago and now on microfilm in the public library.

Knowing, for example, what a busy place Kanuga Conference Center is nowadays, we find it hard to realize it began as simply Kanuga Lake Colony, with perhaps four hundred people in residence during the summer. According to the *Hustler*, residents "will spend certainly not less than $3 apiece each day and they will remain about 100 days." What a boon that was expected to be for Kanuga, and even for the town of Hendersonville. The *Hustler* notes, too: "25 new cottages at Kanuga were already reserved, although they were not yet built, and the capacity of the clubhouse was accordingly greatly increased." At the same time, the new road between Hendersonville and the turn-off to Kanuga was being improved, and, the *Hustler* writes, "this superb highway unfolds to the traveler a panorama of scenic magnificence, at any turn, hardly surpassed anywhere." Never mind summer showers that turned the clay roadbed into muddy ruts.

Hendersonville has long been a summer mecca for residents of New Orleans, many of whom lodged in cottages at the Kanuga Country Club, while others owned cottages on the premises. Although divided into a "New Orleans colony" and a "Charleston colony," camping trips and social events included participants from both places in spite of what they sometimes experienced in order to be available. Many came by train, but one party of fourteen arrived from Jacksonville in three touring cars. They had left

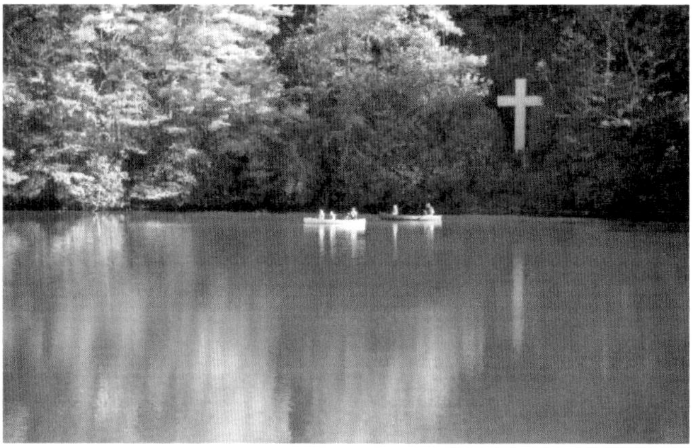

Left: The lake at Kanuga Conferences. *Photo by Terry Ruscin.*

Below: The Dummy Line train ran between downtown Hendersonville and Laurel Park, 1905–12. *Photo courtesy of the Henderson County Genealogical and Historical Society, Inc.*

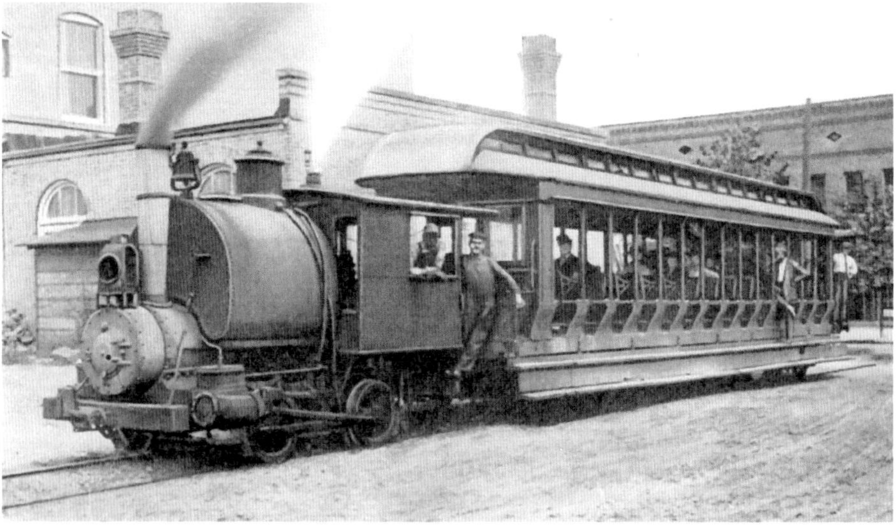

Jacksonville on Monday but were delayed for an entire day by rivers that overflowed their banks during heavy rains and stalled traffic on the major highways. Then, in Hendersonville, the Dummy Line train running from Main Street out Fifth Avenue West to Laurel Park was delayed by water flooding sections of the track.

Meantime, determined to keep Hendersonville and its environs desirable for summer visitors, authorities insisted the streets in town must be kept clean, and could be, they argued, if merchants using them as places to dump their refuse were forbidden to continue that practice.

People who have called Hendersonville their home for a number of years are aware of changes resulting now from progress and growth. They know most of the old landmarks are gone. Familiar names on Main Street—Gregg Hardware, Foster's Fancy Groceries, Holley-Swofford Shoes and many others—have given way to shops with more exotic names. Traffic patterns are changing, but accidents happened even when mule-drawn wagons were the main method of transportation—like the time a heavily loaded wagon collided with a wagon making a routine delivery of groceries. According to the *French Broad Hustler*, the force of the impact was great enough for one wagon to land on top of the other, damaging it severely. But the frantically disconcerted mule teams were soon restored to complacency and, fortunately, without injury. One man who lived on the south end of town and depended on his mule and wagon for transportation had no hands. He wrapped the reins around his wrists and seemed to manage as well as any other driver.

It's interesting to note that, back in the early 1900s, members of a particular organization in session insisted the business of the meeting be carried on with no mention whatever of politics, which, they said, would eliminate what they saw as "a life destroying germ for the organization."

Some wise thoughts have gone into the old *Hustler*. They've made sense across one-hundred-plus years.

Climbing Glassy Mountain

Not a smidgen of air stirred the other day, and the temperature had already sneaked up within a gnat's hair of matching the all-time record. I could look beyond my living room windows and see Glassy Mountain all lush and green, but temptation to climb it was at a standstill, although just looking at it brought back memories of the steep path leading up its northern slope.

I thought about the years a long time ago when we young folks seldom let a week go by without climbing Glassy or Pinnacle. Nowadays, hikers carry bottles of drinking water with them when they expect to be away from home for a while, but we never did. We kept our hands free in order to catch hold of bushes beside the paths to pull ourselves over the rough spots. No one lived on the higher slope of either mountain then, although many years earlier there had been a cabin on the western edge of the top of Glassy. The couple that lived there walked to Argyle to work every morning and then climbed back up the mountain while there was still light enough to see their way. The spring that provided water for the people living in the cabin was still there, with mountain water so clear you could count pebbles on the bottom of it. No one used the spring anymore, but we took turns lying on

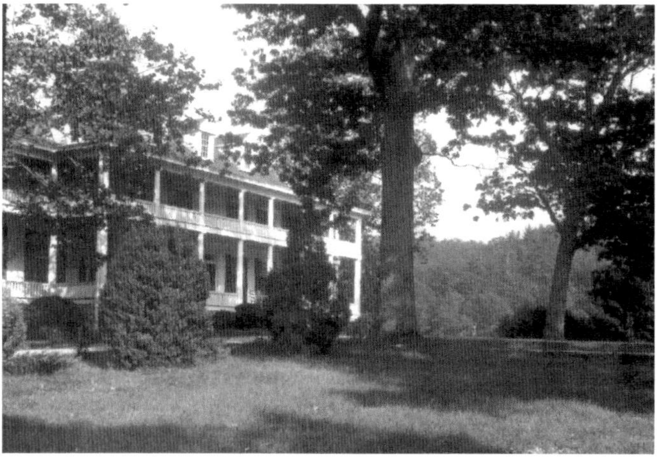

Argyle, the summer home of Judge Mitchell King, Flat Rock. *Photo courtesy of Joseph Bailey Jr.*

our stomachs to drink directly from it—until the time one of us looked up and saw salamanders literally lining the underside of the stone that served as a roof over the spring.

We had another way of quenching our thirst on summer hikes. Sourwood trees grew abundantly on the mountainsides, and sourwood leaves have a tangy flavor if you chew them. You don't want to overdo the time you spend doing it, though, because if you do, you'll find your mouth stained brown, and the color doesn't easily wash off. You have to let it wear off.

While summertime in the mountains can have some mighty hot spells, people from farther south find the elevation invigorating and cooler than in the piedmont area or the Lowcountry. The mother of one of our friends coming each summer from Savannah to Flat Rock always insisted her daughter carry along a sweater to put on when we reached the top of a mountain, no matter how high the temperature was. While the rest of us reveled in the cooling breezes, our friend sat in our summer sunshine swathed in wool.

One thing we took with us to the mountaintops was music. One of our group had a record player, the kind that was built into a big black box and had to be cranked to get it going. Of course, the discs were carried separately and ever so carefully, but the Victrola itself was heavy, and we had to take turns carrying it until we found a spot level enough to keep the needle from sliding out of the grooves in the record that was being played.

Carrying the record player up Glassy or Pinnacle was tedious but well worth the effort, and when all of us sang, whether on key or off—with the recorded musician—residents at the foot of whatever mountain we were on couldn't help knowing we were there.

One of our favorite outings with friends visiting from the flatlands was leading them to Pinnacle Rocks to see the sunrise. How many times we waited for clouds to lift or for an early morning shower to end, I don't recall. I do remember—and vividly—the compensation that came with breakfast at the home of Ellen Stepp on the way back down the mountain.

Roger Richardson Hill's Tomb

There it was, early April, yet snowflakes were coming down every which way before disappearing as soon as they reached the ground. Having no need to be out and about in that kind of weather, I gathered up a significant assortment of items waiting to be seen to and settled in to spend as much of the day with them as would be necessary. Before long, though, the snow flurry stopped, and the sun was doing its best to shine, but the temperature was still far below what I considered adequate for my attending to outdoor matters.

Take, for example, my having put off planting three trays of pansies still on the front porch and in their original containers. They were there to wait until the blossoms had undoubtedly faded, but I could get them out of the way and perhaps make room for more. I had already put sugar water in my hummingbird feeders in case that prospector I've mentioned before happened to come.

So now I was ready to bide my time and just look across to Glassy Mountain, where tall green pines dwarf the vegetation below them. Right now I'm not seeing climbers skirting the rocks halfway up the mountainside and defying not-so-safe footing on the face of them. Instead, they're following a steep trail that runs beside one of those rocks, although a person who's careful enough can ease out far enough to see way off to the top of Jump Off and many miles to each side of it.

Those of us who have long known Glassy Mountain have climbed it maybe as many times to see the sun rise beyond one side of it as to watch glorious sunsets on the other. Sometimes we've watched people rest on the rock that can be seen from my front porch, and with our binoculars it was easy to tell whether they were friends or strangers.

No matter how many times we were at the mountaintop, some of us used to walk a short distance farther to the granite mausoleum of Roger Richardson Hill, who had made arrangements for his brother to ensure his final resting place there. Knowing a failing physical condition would shorten Mr. Hill's life, and that because of it he had made arrangements for his

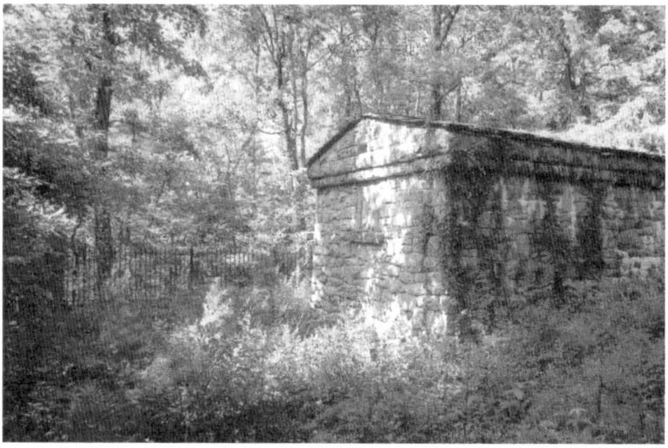

Roger Richardson Hill's mausoleum on Glassy Mountain. *Photo by Terry Ruscin.*

brother to bury him on Glassy, Hill began having a mausoleum built. Many hikers included it in their trips up the mountain, some of them catching their breath while they rested on stones between the wrought-iron railings.

Nowadays, not everyone living even nearby knows of Roger Richardson Hill. But it's worth climbing up the mountain to see the tomb and to think of one to whom the peacefulness of the wooded setting in many ways compensated for physical difficulties he faced during his life. And people notice that the mausoleum doesn't face east as graves ordinarily do. Maybe Mr. Hill's reason for that was his memory of the arid sameness he had left in Texas before coming here. Or was it the view that had drawn him there?

Roger Hill was taken to his final resting place by four horses pulling the wagon that bore his casket. Tall pines still grow on the mountaintop, and the road doesn't run quite near enough the grave for passersby to interrupt the peace and quiet that meant so much to him who had chosen that place. Neither can wind, nor rain, nor an April snow disturb the memories still lingering with the few who once knew the man who felt so called to spend his life, and even his death, in solitude.

WHILE NATURE WAITS

A low gray tomb with ivy 'round its door
And nestled 'mid a grove of tall black pines—
Stern guards that for a century or more
Have whispered elegies among the vines.
It's like a shrine there on the mountaintop,

And all who pass in pleasure or in toil
By some un-meditated order stop
And pray for him who sleeps on alien soil.
Although they knew him not they pray for him,
Then, reverently, they turn toward distant hills,
And stealthily an unknown sadness fills
Their hearts with sorrow and their eyes grow dim…
  Through little chinks where clouds below unfold
  The wheat fields make a cross—a cross of gold.

Upon the snow-clad mountaintop we stand,
A crescent moon has drawn her golden tresses
From o'er the misty veils of shadowed land.
'Tis late, the mists of night fall on our faces,
The valley down below is hid from sight,
But we, and Nature, stand in reverent awe
Because the New Year will be born tonight.
Yon little village now is all aglow.
Its cheerful lights ascend to meet the rays
Of moonlight, and its sleepy people wake
To say goodbye to last year's happy days
And make a toast for Auld Acquaintance sake.
  Then, while Nature waits, all calm and still,
  The New Year steals across the purple hill.

Main Street

If you can remember Main Street in Hendersonville as it was a long time ago—well, before people out there now were around—you know it's basically still the same place it was then, hard as it is to believe. Main Street has always gone through the center of the town, the same as it does now, but King and Church Streets didn't come about until there was enough traffic to warrant putting them in at all. According to Judge Mitchell King, Main Street was wide enough then for a coach drawn by a team of four horses to turn around without backing and then turn again. Mule-drawn wagons were always pulled over to the curb to let traffic by, and the wagon John Anderson rode in was among them.

John lay on a cot in his wagon bed, and when it was parked against a curb on Main Street, friends stopped to pass the time of day with him. No one seemed to know what had incapacitated him, but people accepted him as he was, and with due sympathy. Only when his caregivers passed on did John get up and walk wherever he needed to go. One day while riding with my father down a country road, we came to a man walking at a right good pace ahead of us. My dad told me that was the man I had seen being brought to town lying on a cot in a wagon bed.

Back then, the busiest corner in town was on First Avenue East and Main Street, where Shepherd's store provided Kenny's high-grade coffee, which was ground according to the customer's request, as well as other necessities that couldn't be provided at home. Candies abounded indoors, and at Christmastime the store offered a variety of articles, whether they were hung from the ceiling or were crowded among other items on the shelves.

Because farmers tethered their mules in a vacant lot behind Drake's Store, a watering trough had been put there, but with specific instructions allowing only mules and horses and oxen to drink from it, for that water was not pure enough for human consumption. When an infirmary for people suffering from tuberculosis was set up outside of town, for a long time motorists hesitated even to drive past it for fear of germs they felt might drift their way.

Ten-cent stores thrived on Main Street, especially when F.W. Woolworth built a store between Fourth and Fifth Avenues, displaying a vast assortment

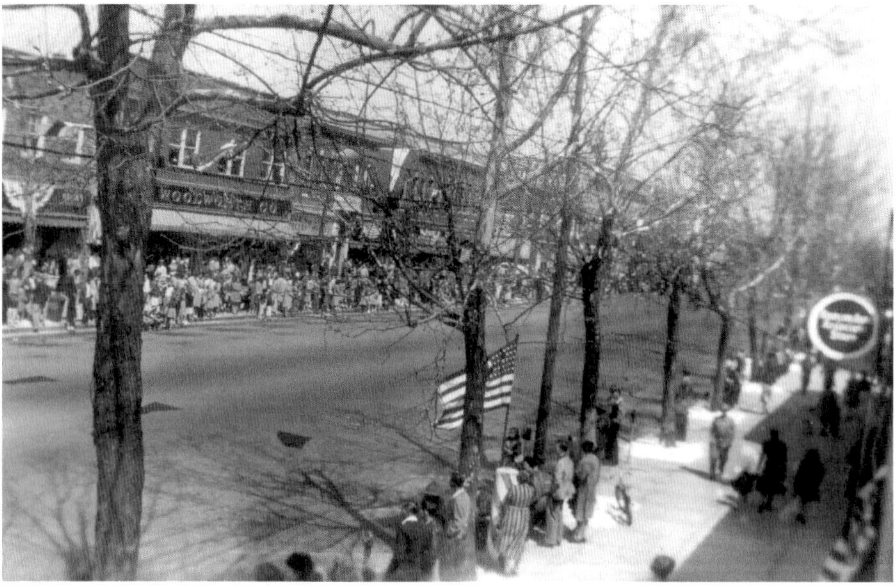

Townsfolk await the 1947 Henderson County King Apple Parade on Hendersonville's Main Street (F.W. Woolworth is in the background). *Photo courtesy of the Henderson County Genealogical and Historical Society, Inc.*

of necessary items costing only a dime apiece. People flocked to Woolworth's to buy and often just to look as they entered in front of a particularly popular display of a row of candies in large containers with glass windows facing the aisle. One of those containers held slabs of Hershey's chocolate, some of them weighing up to ten pounds, and they had to be replaced many times, for a dime's worth of savory milk chocolate was a special treat while you waited for your dad to close his office for the day and take you home if you lived too far from town to walk.

The *Carolina Special* starting up the mountain climb from Tryon to Saluda called attention to our town. Facing the railroad at the Tryon station, a great sign stood, informing travelers where to find accommodations in Hendersonville. Obviously, the manager of one of our town's hotels had put up the sign.

Of course, all of this effort resulted in convincing businessmen of the dire need of paving certain streets. The matter caused such frustration on the part of one of those persons that he offered to pay a third of the cost himself.

When I ride through town now with a traffic light on every corner and go on along Church Street, I think about the Noterman House that stood for years before it was taken down so the street could be opened for traffic. I remember young folks skating all over town, but I never see skates anymore. My sister and I had one pair of skates between us, and she, being my elder, claimed the right-hand one, although neither of us was left-handed.

But as far as the town itself is concerned, change has come with the times. It's good we have recollections, though, if only to remind us of the way things used to be.

Remembering Old Times

Something like forty-two years ago, I happened to stop in the newspaper office on some trivial matter, and coming out I balanced on the toes of one foot long enough to say "Howdy" to the editor. He responded quickly by waving without even looking up. Apparently he'd heard I'd given a spiel at some organization, but he didn't mention it. He kept on writing, but he said, "I know you have notes. Let me see them." I copied them over so they would be legible and dropped them off at his desk. The next thing I knew, they were coming back to me in the newspaper. "I need some more," he said.

That went on for four or five years. One day, I phoned him with marked timidity to ask if I could possibly get a little fee for my columns, although I don't know when I have enjoyed any task so much. Remembering old times proved a pure delight, and because of my vintage I could go back to people and experiences that are history now. I could remember seeing mule teams tethered behind Shepherd's store on the eastern corner of First Avenue. And if I'd had a dime to squander, I could have paid it to join others seeing "Fats" McCall when he was driven to town and parked on Main Street so his friends could look in to pass the time of day with him. He spent idle moments with friends whom he supposed valued his opinions.

I could see how the women folks dressed up to go on Main Street, and on some of the corners men preached blood and thunder to the wayward, one of them, especially, alternately springing in the air and then crouching on his knees.

During the school year, some of us walked on to our homes south of town. One of our friends rode partway with us on her pony she had tethered behind the school while she attended classes. The present Hendersonville High School building wasn't there yet. Upper classmen met in a big frame house in the center of what's now Church Street. When my dad came to Sixth Avenue on Church Street and could see all the way to Caswell, he said, "Look at the automobiles!"—seeing three of them between there and the railroad track at the end of the street. Down there a fellow was often working

M.M. Shepherd Store, circa early 1900s. This building—downtown Hendersonville's first—in later years was called Drake's Store. It also housed Hendersonville's first post office, first drugstore, a photographer's studio, a barroom, a produce market and an infirmary. The building no longer stands. *Photo courtesy of John Paul Jones.*

in his yard. Toward Church Street, his window shades were raised only a few inches because he said he didn't want his wife looking out the window when she had other things to do.

Ours was a sleepy little town then, but it came to life in the summer when the South Carolinians and Floridians came to enjoy the mountain air. It seemed to bring new life to them for the summer months. Doctors were particularly busy, though, some of the South Carolina ladies being very exacting about the times house calls should be made. Doctors arranged their house calls accordingly so as not to interrupt the ladies' midday dinner hours, and the doctors' dinners were postponed until the house calls were over.

Only in autumn could my dad take time off. That was when he went to his mountain cabin with a man to cook for him and a thickly stuffed bunk to sleep on. He washed in a pan of ice-cold water from the creek, and he rested indoors by a roaring fire. Happiness was the primitive life he spent enjoying in the mountains.

The cabin is in ruins now, and a paved road leads almost to it. People have moved into the community, and a new way of life has taken over. Forty-two years have brought many differences, but we remember the old ways.

Octagon Soap

A recent conversation worked itself around to a link between a particular railroad track and a bar of soap. The track needed no explanation, for it's still visible enough, although seldom used. And I supposed the soap was as familiar to other people as it is to me. Not only was I wrong, but also the matter of combining two such diverse subjects into one discussion did seem rather unusual.

I couldn't believe some of the people with whom I was talking have grown to the age of grandparents without knowing there's such a thing as an eight-sided bar of soap, which, with the corners cut off, accounts for its being called Octagon Soap. There's a coupon on the wrapper, which has always been a benefit to housewives who can't resist a bonus. Essential as Octagon Soap has proven to be to southern households, I supposed it was indispensable elsewhere as well, loosening dirt from working men's overalls, lathering hands that had come in contact with poison ivy and, during the years Mary had come down from her home on Pinnacle Mountain to look after my sister and me when we were children, bathing us with Octagon Soap, which gave us the benefit of a milder soap than the homemade lye variety Mary used on inanimate objects.

She used the Octagon so freely on our fair skin that in later years someone told me we always looked as if we had been scrubbed with Sapolio. I've never known what Sapolio was, but I do know that, more times than I care to count, my skin has bent hypodermic needles, and one even broke in two on its way in, thanks to the toughening process of Octagon Soap.

While I was remembering that soap, thoughts came to mind of the old trains laboring up the grade from Melrose to Saluda. It's not as strange an association as you might think—a particular bar of soap and, say, a freight train.

Naturally, the climb was easier when diesel engines replaced the steam ones, but for a time there were folks who vowed a diesel couldn't make the grade. One day, some fellows sitting on a shaded bench on Saluda's Main Street were watching for the train yet vowing it could never make the grade up from Melrose with that little engine pulling but no "helper" pushing. They couldn't believe it when they saw the diesel come in sight with one hundred freight cars right behind it.

What the fellows didn't know was that the grade wasn't the only reason the old steam engines now and then had a hard time climbing up from Melrose. Would you believe half a bar of Octagon Soap was responsible for it? You know how a bunch of boys are always looking for something to do, and more often than not, they think up a prank that puzzles the grownups but doesn't cause real harm. Inconvenience, yes. And certain ingenuity spurs it on. That was what happened when some boys looking for what they thought would be fun broke a bar of Octagon Soap in two and then rubbed the cut end along little stretches of railroad track. Engine wheels lost their traction, and sometimes the train had to roll back to Melrose to get a fresh start up the grade to Saluda.

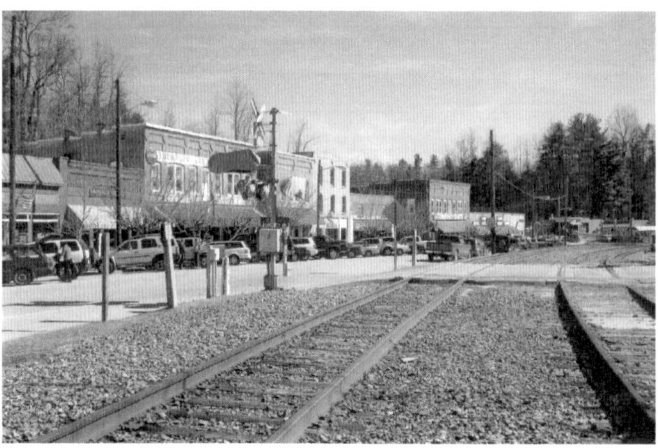

Saluda's Main Street.
Photo by Terry Ruscin.

It's surprising to find so many people nowadays who never heard of Octagon Soap when just a couple of square inches on the end of half a bar of it could have such an impact on the Southern Railway system.

Old-time Logging

People nowadays tend to think of the way things were done one hundred years ago as old-timey. Never mind that, as long as the particular job was accomplished. What they really need to recognize is the ingenuity of those early settlers who carved a homeland out of a mountain wilderness, not with steam shovels and tractors, but with axes and crosscut saws. No wonder they gave their early settlements names like Bad Fork, Tear Britches Ridge, Cut Throat Gap, Corn Cob Mountain and Cold Knob.

When those early settlers needed lumber, there was an abundance of it—millions of feet of full-grown virgin timber in the forests that flourished on our mountains back then. In the 1920s, the sound of no woodsman's axe had ever echoed through the primeval forest near the foot of Whiteside Mountain. So when the settlers came and needed lumber for their houses, their problem was not a shortage of trees but the matter of getting them out to the early lumber mills, for they had to be snaked out with a team of oxen doing the pulling. Nor were there roads over which the timber could be hauled. So the old-timers came up with the idea of building temporary dams across creeks that flowed through the forests, and each one of the dams

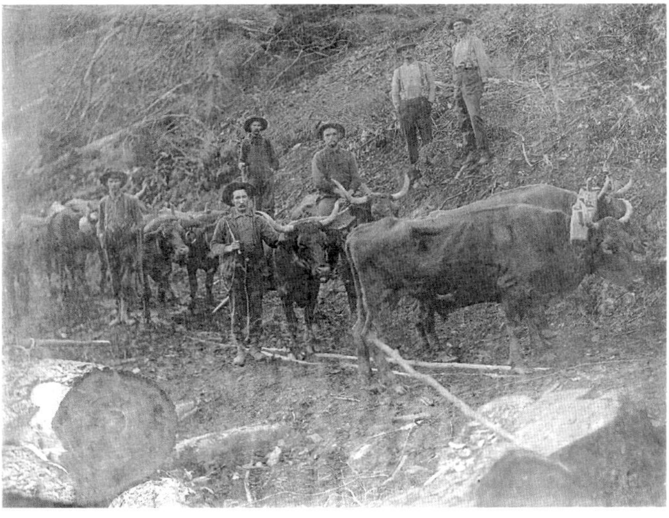

Oxen hauling a load of logs in Pisgah Forest, early 1900s. *Photo courtesy of John Paul Jones.*

backed up water over several acres of land. If the timber to be taken out was to belong to more than one person, the initials of each one of the several owners were burned on whatever logs would be theirs. Then the logs were left behind the dams that had been holding the water within the creeks in order to keep the logs from washing away.

Logjams resulted, but in time spring freshets came, bringing with them the need to set the logs free. So the temporary dams were blown up, and enough empty space resulted for the heavy rains to wash through, taking the logs with them. Mills River, for example, flooded across flat bottomlands, taking with it logs that were covered with mud, washing them out into the farmlands and clogging the surging waters of the French Broad River that flowed through the acres.

The situation was such that less than half of the valuable poplar timber could be saved and sawed into lumber. The rest of it eventually washed from one river into another all the way to the Mississippi, there to begin its final journey to the Gulf of Mexico, where it would be loaded onto ships bound for distant ports.

I've never seen it written, but it must be recorded somewhere how long a poplar log might have spent on its journey from the mountains of Western North Carolina to the Gulf of Mexico. And when you think of the distance those logs traveled, and of the numbers of people they washed within sight of, you can't help wondering if all of them reached their intended destination or if an occasional one was dragged to shore to serve some immediate purpose.

People one hundred years ago would find it hard to believe how much help there is in the equipment and machinery available for getting difficult jobs done nowadays. Ingenuity keeps showing up, though, and someday in the distant future people will think back on the ways we have now of making things easy for us. They'll probably consider us downright old-timey.

OLD-TIME HENDERSONVILLE

You might say our founding fathers went about it backwards. The tree-lined streets of today's progressive town of Hendersonville have come a long way since Judge Mitchell King donated land on Chinquapin Hill for a courthouse to be built when there wasn't even a town in the midst of the scattered settlements already established.

While no one prefers the rapid approach of personal antiquity, fortunate are those in whose memories highlights in the development of our town

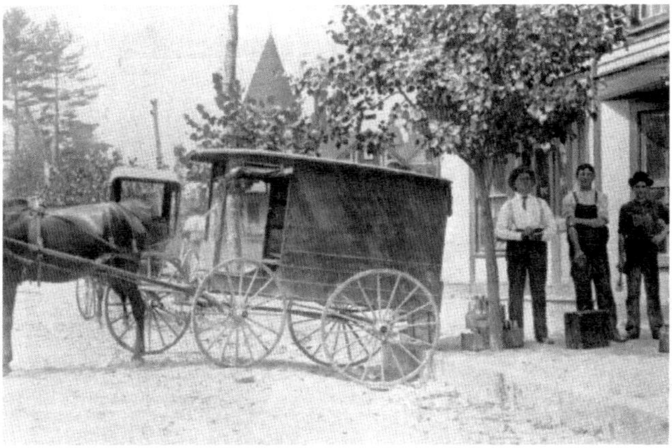

Horses, mules and oxen were familiar conveyances in the downtown Hendersonville of yesteryear. Pictured is the L.W. Walker Bottling Plant, on the south side of Seventh Avenue East. *Photo by Floy Justus Davidson, courtesy of the Henderson County Genealogical and Historical Society, Inc.*

stand out, and looking back on them tells us things that bring alive a history that people moving in from all parts of our nation need to know.

For example, many of those newcomers have not yet read that until the mid-1930s, in spite of an increasing number of automobiles, mule-drawn wagons still brought farmers to town on Saturdays. The majority of the wagons were parked on South King Street, and the mules were unhitched and tethered in the lot while the men attended to matters in town.

When an epidemic of yellow fever raged in Florida, patients were brought to an infirmary that had been set up for them on that lot, but when a cure for yellow fever was found, the infirmary was no longer needed and was taken down.

In winter, a potbellied stove inside our town's first store offered warmth to men who came to town in all kinds of weather, sitting on unprotected wagon seats whatever the temperature out of doors.

Our town started out with just one traffic light on Main Street. It was on the corner of Fourth Avenue and Main Street, and because the post office was half a block down Fourth Avenue West, that was understandably the busiest street in town.

A fellow known as "Pretty Daddy" spent many hours sitting on a green bench at the corner of Fourth Avenue and Main Street "how-doing" people passing by.

Summertime Saturdays brought people into town to do their trading, and they would sit on benches along the sidewalks to chat with one another. Special attractions were brought to Main Street, like a fellow who tried to climb the courthouse wall and the farmer who owned what was said to be the largest hog in the world. It weighed a little more than a ton, and folks could pay a dime to peer into the bed of a truck and see it right on Main Street.

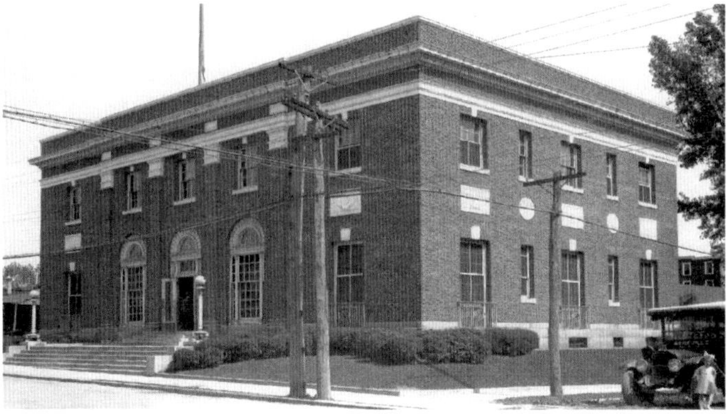

The Federal Building, formerly the Hendersonville Post Office (1914–65), on the corner of Fourth Avenue West and Church Street. *Photo courtesy of the Henderson County Genealogical and Historical Society, Inc.*

Well-known bands and orchestras came to Hendersonville in the summer, when our tourist season was in full swing. Laurel Park Lake and Rainbow Lake provided beaches, and for a time a trolley ran out Fifth Avenue from Main Street to Laurel Park. Long after the trolley was discontinued, the tracks remained, but by no means in a straight line. Our motorists of that time could tell you the tracks were definitely not level with the pavement and had to be crisscrossed all the way out Fifth Avenue.

Flappers drove up and down Main Street with the canvas tops of their cars down and the rumble seats invitingly open.

Dime stores must have done well back then, for we had three of them. The favorite of most of us, though, was Woolworth's.

And we had two theaters. One of them went for westerns, and I saw most of them with a cousin who loved them, but he was so nearsighted we had to sit almost on the front row, which really put us into the action. *Titanic* was the last movie I saw, but I'll get to another when the right one comes along.

It seems a long time ago that mule teams came to town on Saturdays. A lot of changes have come about in what we do and how we go about it, but what a privilege it has been for those of us who have watched it all take place.

THE ANGEL IN OAKDALE CEMETERY

There I was, the only person standing among those hundreds of gravestones in Oakdale Cemetery. I was glad no one happened along with condolences in mind or to ask if the plot I was looking at contained some of my relatives because it has no connection at all with my family and would likely have raised all the more curiosity about my being there.

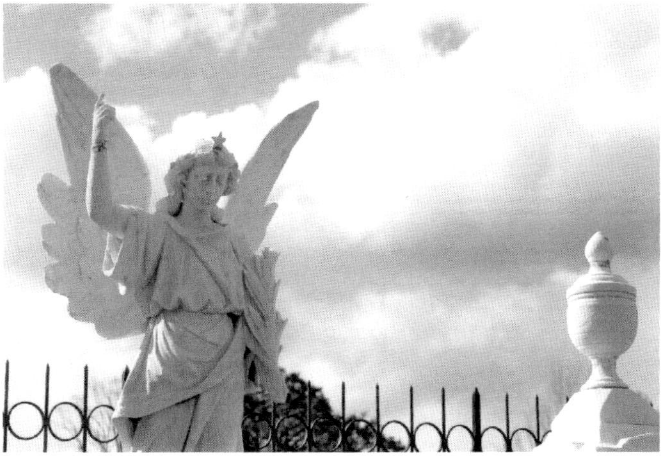

"Wolfe's Angel" on the Johnson family plot, Oakdale Cemetery, Hendersonville. *Photo by Terry Ruscin.*

What had drawn me to the grave site was the fact that it's the one on which stands Thomas Wolfe's storied angel, and I was there on behalf of some third- and fourth-grade pupils I'd been asked to talk to rather briefly about the angel. Not that they were planning to read the book yet, young as they were, but they'll remember it and someday they'll know the story. I knew that meantime those young folks would have questions, and I would be expected to have answers.

So there I stood beside the angel that had actually been housed in Asheville, where it remained for a time on the porch of the shop owned by Thomas Wolfe's father. According to records, when Margaret E. Johnson [Mrs. H.F. Johnson]—whose name is on the gravestone—died in 1905, her children purchased the angel, had "OUR MOTHER" carved at the base of it and moved it onto her grave. Her husband's stone, labeled "OUR FATHER," stands beside it, and the grave of their son, Leander, whom many of us knew at the Historic Johnson Farm on Haywood Road, is also in the Oakdale plot.

Various misconceptions have arisen over the years as to the authenticity of the angel, especially when certain other cities across the country have claimed possession of the real angel, and people in some of those places have insisted the monument in Oakdale is a copy of the real one in a graveyard in an entirely different town. The claims have been proven false. The late Sadie Patton, for example, was sure she had found reason to believe the angel in Oakdale Cemetery unmistakably marks the grave of Margaret Johnson. Mrs. Patton bases her belief on the fact that in *Look Homeward, Angel*, Thomas Wolfe mentions the condition of the angel's feet—the "phthisical" state of toes that have begun to draw and become gnarled from the ravages of tuberculosis. There's a hint of such toes on the feet of the angel in Oakdale

Cemetery, and tuberculosis was a common disease at that time. So I judged my mission complete and my answers ready for whatever questions would come from the third and fourth graders.

As I drove away, though, I remembered that years ago I had seen a certain vault near the angel that had square glass prisms across the top. The person buried there [the "Sunshine Lady," Leila Davidson Hansell] was one of the people who had died of tuberculosis, and her request had been that she be buried where the sun could shine on her all day. Curiosity drew people to the site, and small children living near the cemetery saw them peering through the prisms to glimpse the remains of the departed and to comment on the beautiful auburn hair draped across her shoulders. The children knew the view was clearer if dust were removed from the glass prisms in the vault's lid, so they rushed from their nearby houses to the grave, bringing glasses of water to sell for a dime a glass to the visitors. Eventually, though, the prisms were blocked out in respect for the departed.

And if the foot condition of Thomas Wolfe's angel bears any resemblance to our "hammer toes," many people have that much in common with her.

"DANCINGEST TOWN IN AMERICA"

Some of us remember when Hendersonville was called the "dancingest town in America," and we know it had good reason for the sobriquet. It was a long time ago, and well-known bands came to play for dances at our summer resorts. Word spread quickly, and summer visitors from south of us—admittedly coming for more than just the refreshing climate compared to that of sun-parched South Carolina, Georgia and Florida—doubled the population that was here during much of the rest of the year. Hal Kemp was one of them who brought his band, and Jan Garber brought a number of musicians. Their members found lodging at various places in and around town, and a favorite site for the entertainment they provided was at the casino that used to be at Laurel Park Lake, where people gathered to swim, picnic and relax on a sandy beach.

On our way home from a vacation in Florida one spring, we stopped at a roadside café. Seeing we were strangers, one person and another spoke to us in their friendly manner, always asking the usual "Where are you from?" When we told them, each one mentioned having spent time here, some of them a whole summer. One of them said he had heard Jan Garber play for one of our dances. I told him I remembered when that was and that I had seen the

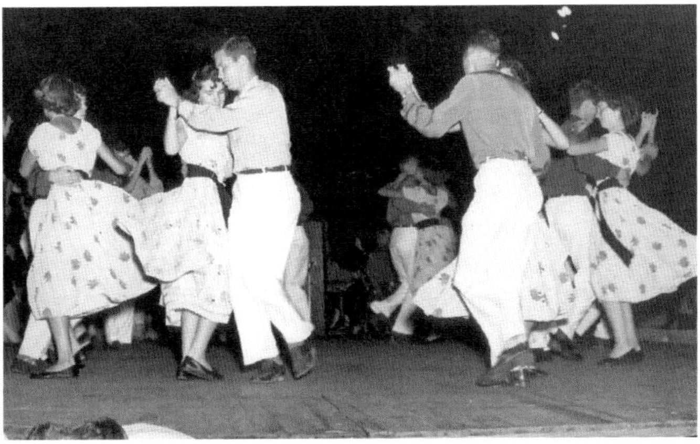

Dancing in "dancingest" Hendersonville, people and location unidentified. *Photo courtesy of the Henderson County Genealogical and Historical Society, Inc.*

musicians a number of times on the street and was still chuckling about the way several members had chosen an unprecedented—in Hendersonville, at least—stunt to attract attention. They had walked to Main Street and back to Laurel Park wearing their pajamas. They unquestionably accomplished their purpose, while at the same time horrifying certain dignified citizens who happened to see them. As well as I remember, they were not invited back for future engagements.

We had no buses then, but from the corner of Fifth Avenue West and Main Street, tracks were laid for the trolley we once had. They turned on out to the pavilion at Laurel Park Lake and then across Fifth Avenue to Crystal Spring, where Floridians heading home filled jugs with mountain water to take with them. That particular railroad was called the Dummy Line simply because the train had no place to turn around, coming forward to Main Street and backing to Laurel Park. Understandably, it ran only in the summer when Laurel Park was in use. And, according to Frank L. FitzSimons Sr., it would have made a round trip every half hour between nine o'clock in the morning and eleven o'clock at night if it hadn't often jumped the track at that modest curve on Fifth Avenue just before the road starts up Jump Off Mountain. Several men could easily pick it up, though, and set it upright again, which was fortunate when it happened so often.

Recently, a friend drove me past the area where the lakebed used to be. Modern houses are there now, but the driver, who had not heard its history, said the terrain looked as though a lake might have been there at one time. So I told her about days gone by and about the tall metal slide swimmers used to zoom down and make mighty splashes as they hit the water. She couldn't believe the changes that have taken place; nor had she ever heard that the city had once provided a public swimming pool on Washington Street. She wondered what the reaction would be to the popular swimwear today.

But times change. So do people and customs. It's worth looking back, though, and remembering.

PLACES OF INTEREST IN FLAT ROCK

Some of Flat Rock has more artistic history than may be known by many of its residents who haven't been there since days gone by. The Old Mill Playhouse is one of them, and many from its earlier years [as Rhett's Mill and, later, a venue for Robroy Farquhar's Vagabond Players] have become no longer commonplace. One of them, for example, goes back to when Hollywood was represented here many years ago by Warner Brothers, which, for a time, took over property that later became Crail Farm and some years earlier had been the summer retreat of Mitchell King of Atlanta, a grandson of Judge Mitchell King.

The Warners had enlarged the house in order to send members of their casts to enjoy relaxation in the quiet wooded area. Then the playhouse was built a short distance from it, keeping members of the casts close together. When the Warners eventually moved away, the house and property were sold to a family who lived there whenever they could be away from their chain of cafeterias in neighboring towns. At the same time, in Flat Rock they maintained well-kept chicken houses filled with white leghorn hens that provided eggs for the cafeterias.

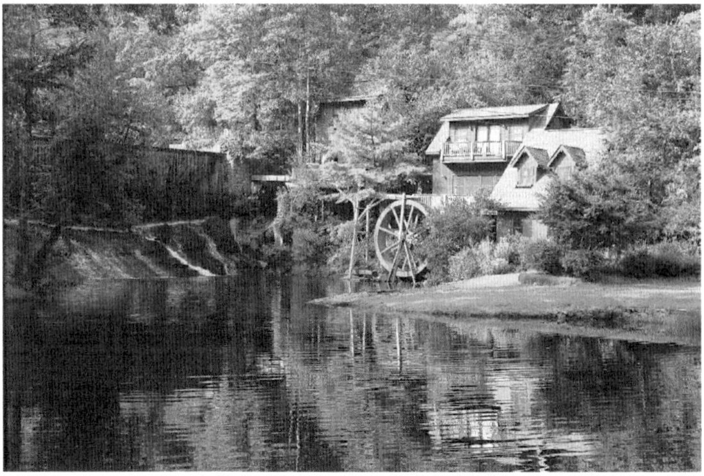

Site of Rhett's Mill and the Old Mill Playhouse. *Photo by Terry Ruscin.*

The cafeterias did not use eggs that had become cracked, for whatever reason and however slightly. We neighbors were able to buy them at minimum prices, so I always had several dozen on top of my refrigerator. When my family went to Florida for spring vacations, cracked eggs went with us, as did many threats that lack of space for feet was no excuse for dangerously crowding the eggs. Perish the thought of putting them in the trunk, where not a spare inch of space was available anyway, along with all the beach paraphernalia. But how our beach neighbors envied our frugality for having eggs at twenty-five or so cents a dozen!

We were always back home in time for the opening performance at the Old Mill Playhouse and for an opportunity to meet the players. Some were experienced in summer stock; others sought experience and happily expected to find it at Flat Rock. What they had not expected was that when the lights were dimmed, a bat was likely to swoop among them. Ladies squealed and ducked their heads; men waved their hats. Blinded by a sudden light in the auditorium, a bat once paused on a lady's hands, which she had folded on her lap. Her reaction did not fall short of expectations.

With it all, the Old Mill Playhouse maintained its steadily increasing popularity. Then one member went on to Hollywood for a role in *Planet of the Apes*; others went elsewhere. I still think about Mitchell King, though, who came from Atlanta frequently before the playhouse was built. How he enjoyed the country atmosphere and the novelty, for him, to be away from the sounds of traffic and city hubbub, shelling ears of corn grown on his Flat Rock property and tossing the kernels to ducks paddling on a pond he had built just for them.

The name Crail Farm, having come from Argyllshire in Scotland, where Judge Mitchell King's forebears had lived, is no longer used for the present area of modern dwellings in Flat Rock. Year-round houses are there now where a green meadow used to be.

A paved road leads past what used to be the Old Mill Playhouse, where mill wheels turn as they have done throughout Flat Rock's history.

Little Charleston of the Mountains

Every other July, we look forward to the annual tour of Flat Rock's historic homes. Surely we old-timers haven't grown so accustomed to some of our surroundings that we tend to overlook their significance in our midst.

The Flat Rock Inn, once known as Five Oaks, was on one year's list of places to be seen partly because of certain structural features. For example,

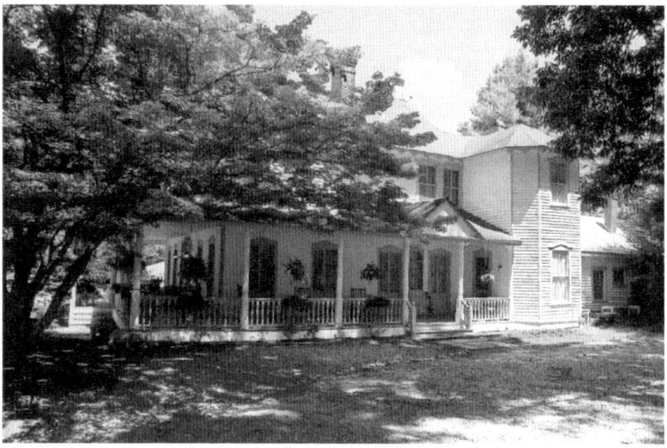

The Flat Rock Inn, formerly Five Oaks, Flat Rock. *Photo by Terry Ruscin.*

did you know that the spacious Flat Rock Inn was a private home for many years before it became an inn?

Robert Withers Memminger, a son of Christopher Gustavus Memminger—first secretary of the Confederate Treasury—served as an officer on General Robert E. Lee's staff until he received an injury that plagued him for the rest of his life. As a result, he became an Episcopal priest, and when duties permitted, he spent time at Five Oaks, now the Flat Rock Inn.

In 1909, Five Oaks became the property of Thomas Grimshawe, an Englishman temporarily in Canada, where he had made a loan of a considerable amount to a friend. When payment was due, the borrower offered Mr. Grimshawe a choice: he could give him the required amount, or he could deed broad acreage to him in a Western North Carolina wilderness already known to South Carolinians as an ideal summer resort. Thomas Grimshawe chose the land, and he and his wife and family of several little girls journeyed from Canada to the area we know today as Cashiers. For the few scattered settlers, a post office was built—one small room on the edge of the main road. It was said to be the smallest post office in the United States.

You can go now to where the old homeplace was and see the yard where the little Grimshawe children played. But you see also, in the graveyard of Cashier's Episcopal church, the graves of those little girls. While Mr. Grimshawe was back in Canada on a business trip, an epidemic of diphtheria swept through the North Carolina mountain area. With no rector available, Mrs. Grimshawe herself read the funeral service at the grave of each of her little girls.

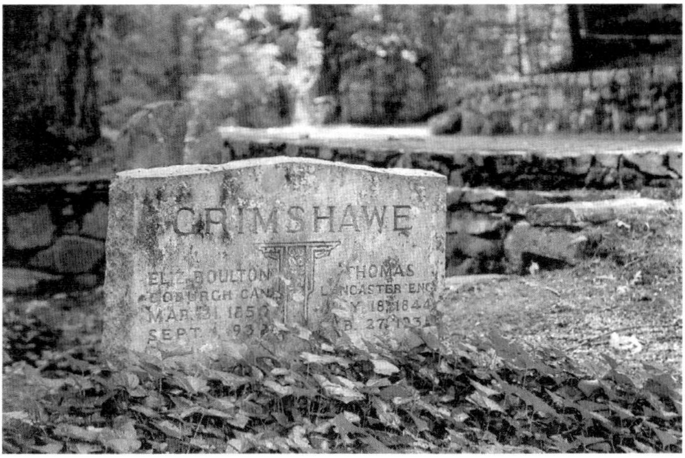

Grimshawe Plot at the Episcopal Church of St. John in the Wilderness, Flat Rock. Others of the Grimshawes' children lie buried in the family's plot at the Episcopal Church of the Good Shepherd in Cashiers. *Photo by Terry Ruscin.*

Mr. and Mrs. Grimshawe moved over to Flat Rock to spend the rest of their lives. There, another daughter and a son were born to them and were lifetime Flat Rock residents.

My father particularly enjoyed Mr. Thomas Grimshawe's company and sometimes took him along on house calls made to patients in the four corners of Henderson County. He not only found Mr. Grimshawe an interesting person, but he also had to confess to his amusement at watching the old gentleman vent his eagerness to see the sights along the roadsides. For with practiced dexterity Mr. Grimshawe managed his monocle, the only monocle used in Flat Rock or probably in all of Henderson County. Raising his head slightly upward and anchoring the monocle between upper and lower eyelids, he peered through it for what he must have considered a clearer view of the object of interest. Why he chose to favor only one eye instead of using a pair of spectacles, he is no longer here to explain.

When the Flat Rock house tour is in full swing in July, people will take note of architecture and design and the assurance of getting relief from the summer heat and mosquitoes of the South Carolina Lowcountry. Hopefully they'll remember Thomas Grimshawe, his wife and others who used to make Flat Rock, "little Charleston of the mountains," come alive from May into September.

Little River Road

In 1926, my father bought property on Little River Road in the heart of Flat Rock. Miss Cherry Morton, a first cousin of the Norton sisters of Louisville, built a large summer house called Laurelhurst in the late 1800s. The Norton sisters had purchased adjoining property, formerly the Count Marie Joseph de Choiseul's "Castle," now Chanteloup. There the count's family had lived year-round while he attended to consular duties between Charleston and Paris. Laurelhurst was occupied just in summer.

Until the early 1900s, the Greenville Highway (N.C. 225) was the only paved road through the residential community of Flat Rock. Deep ruts in the red clay of side roads often required chains and even then were difficult to get through. At times, passing another car was impossible without backing to a wider spot, which challenged even the most experienced driver. When a winter storm brought a deep snow during Captain Ellison Adger Smyth's illness at Connemara—his Flat Rock home and later that of Carl Sandburg—his doctor drove to where Little River Road turns west from N.C. 225. There, Smyth's farm manager met him with a team of horses and a wagon to take him on to the patient.

After World War II, people from various parts of the country began building year-round houses along Little River Road. When driving, they frequently found themselves directly behind a wagon drawn by a team of oxen taking a man to or from his daily job. With no room to get by, the motorists had no choice but to follow at the oxen's pace.

For a number of years, Pheasant Branch flowed out of the woods and crossed the surface of Little River Road. The stream was too shallow to cause any inconvenience, and Abraham Kuykendall's gold, which was said to have been buried somewhere along Pheasant Branch, has never washed out as far as we know. Nowadays, the stream flows underneath the pavement and out of sight of the many motorists passing by too quickly to notice it.

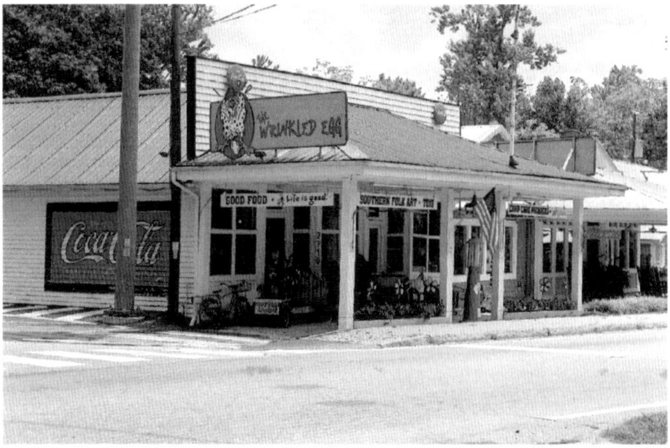

The Wrinkled Egg, formerly Peace's Grocery, Flat Rock. *Photo by Terry Ruscin.*

We have to admit ice can be a problem on what we now call "Sandburg's Hill" leading to Highway 225. Once my car kept slipping backward on that slope, so I left it at the bottom, out of the way of other vehicles, and walked on to the highway to take the bus into town. When I came back, the car was waiting for me at the top of the hill. Someone who recognized it and knew how to start it without the key had done me the favor of driving it up to level ground.

People often walked along Little River Road a number of years ago, some of them going to Peace's Grocery, now called the Wrinkled Egg because a hen in the lot behind the store laid eggs with a calcium deficiency that caused the shells to wrinkle. Other people hoped to be picked up by someone driving to town. Carl Sandburg took walks well past midnight, when he had the road to himself and could concentrate on what he would be writing the next day. Few people saw him at such a late hour, but my husband, Joe, on his way to or from night calls at the hospital, occasionally did.

When Mr. Sandburg asked me if I could type "with as many as two fingers," and if I were free in the afternoons to type his manuscript for *Remembrance Rock*, I confessed I had used a typewriter less than half a dozen times. He hired me anyway and afforded me the rare opportunity of being in the presence of that great mind at work. When Joe came home from a year of military duty in Japan, I turned the typewriter over to a friend who knew how to use it, and she did so for the next twenty years. The one advantage I'd had over her was that my house was within walking distance of Connemara, and once in a snow too deep to drive through I was able to go on to my job. Mr. Sandburg asked if I might spend the night so we could continue working in the evening. I said I would be glad to, but when we finished supper he picked up his guitar and began to sing. We forewent an evening of work for a

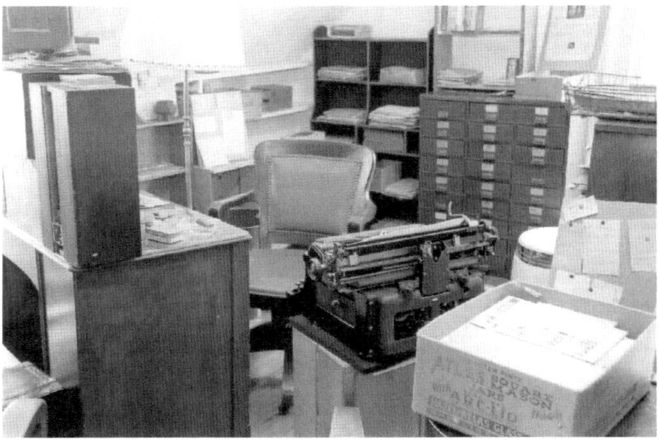

Carl Sandburg's upstairs office at Connemara. *Photo by Terry Ruscin.*

delightful one of music. Then, in spite of a pair of Mrs. Sandburg's pajamas needing to be three sizes larger for me, I spent a restful night and was up the next morning in time to walk home for breakfast.

In the 1960s, the Highway Department paved Little River Road. Work was begun in March, one of the wettest Marches on record. Words can't describe the mud and the sound of automobile engines grinding to pull out of it. The fervent hope of motorists was that no oncoming car would appear. Throughout that month, a bulldozer waited at the top of Sandburg's Hill with a driver on call in case Dr. Joe had to be towed out to the highway on his way to attend to an emergency.

Some residents were not in favor of paving Little River Road. They liked the shaded, curving drive and were afraid it would become a speedway, which it already was for one man who made milk deliveries while standing up in his truck and taking curves and bumps at such speed the bottles rattled ominously, yet none of them ever broke.

Before television's intrusion on our thoughts and actions, we sat on the piazza on summer evenings. Little River Road passed the far end of our driveway, slightly less than a half mile from our house. There were times traffic seemed to pick up after dark, and although headlights could warn other travelers that a car was approaching, at a certain place a horn sounded, not with just a simple toot, but with a somewhat elongated one. Presently, another horn sounded from a short distance behind the first one.

I'd been told about signals, so I knew a "lookout" car was ahead. Where a side road comes into Little River Road, a revenuer might have been waiting, watching, and the horn indicated the intersection was clear. The driver, making a delivery of moonshine, then let the lookout man know he was

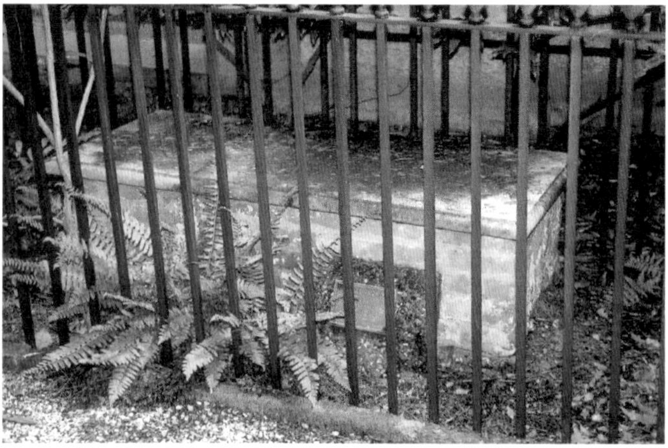

James Brown's tomb (a former repository for moonshine) at the Episcopal Church of St. John in the Wilderness, Flat Rock. *Photo by Terry Ruscin.*

heading on to his appointed destination. When he arrived, he would likely stop short of the house, turn off his lights and, in the darkness, imitate the call of some specified creature of the woods. In due time, business would be completed and, once more, without the revenuers being aware of it.

It is said that the grave of James Brown [a trumpeter with the Royal Scots Greys who fought at the Battle of Waterloo] beside the Episcopal Church of St. John in the Wilderness was once a drop-off place for mountain moonshine. That can't be known for sure because no records exist to prove it. But Little River Road has played an important role in Flat Rock's history, a twofold history that's well known by many of the old-timers.

The Golf Course at Connemara

No one is alive now who saw the golf course being built at Captain Ellison Adger Smyth's Connemara in Flat Rock, surely one of the earliest golf courses in Henderson County.

Between 1900 and 1906, workmen on the Connemara farm built it, and they did it without machinery, with oxen, horses, drag pans, shovels, mattocks and hand-pulled rollers or packers. The term "greens" is misleading when it refers to a golf course, because what should have been green, and would have indicated grass, was not grass at all. It was packed sand and clay. Although the course was on the slope between Smyth's house and Little River Road, the greens were level, being cut into the slope where necessary. And since each green was about twenty-five feet in diameter, with the hole or cup in the center, creating it with the meager equipment available required considerable labor.

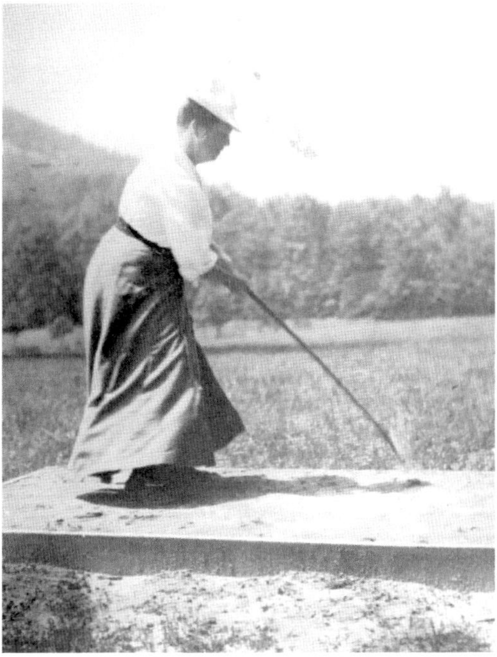

Annie Pierce Smyth Blake plays golf on Henderson County's first course at Connemara. *Photo by Barber, courtesy of Julianne Heggoy and Carl Sandburg Home NHS.*

Power mowers had not yet come into use, and grass was lush on the hillside. A member of the Smyth family tells me that Connemara did have a one-horse mower with a three-foot cut, but the best way to keep the fairways open when grass became several inches long was to use them as pasturage for sheep and cattle when the need arose. Thus the course was kept in shape with the small one-horse mower and the farm animals grazing.

As they do today, two lakes added to the beauty of Connemara's property during Captain Smyth's ownership, the "big" or "front" lake at the foot of the hill in front of the house and the "small" or "back" lake between the house and Little River Road, as the Smyth family called them. The tee boxes golfers stood on to drive were apparently six by ten feet, made with sides of twelve-inch boards and filled with sand. On page 168 in the book *Hendersonville and Henderson County*, Jody Barber's photograph shows a member of Captain Smyth's family standing on a tee box as she prepares to drive. Her golfing attire is particularly interesting.

Players started from a tee near the front of Connemara and drove to the first green or hole that was near the small lake. Next, the player drove on the other side of the lake to the second green. Holes three to eight circled through the pasture facing Little River Road and across the creek near the barn and back to the eighth hole, which was between the lake and the road. To complete the round, the player again drove on the other side of the lake to what was originally the first hole but had necessarily become the ninth one.

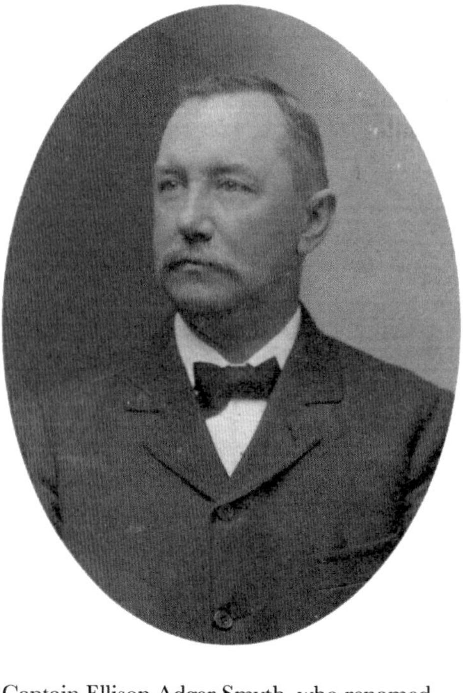

Captain Ellison Adger Smyth, who renamed C.G. Memminger's Rock Hill as Connemara. *Photo courtesy of Julianne Heggoy.*

Golf clubs of that era fitted into a small golf bag, and for many players there were only three clubs—a driver, a putter and a "spoon" that lifted the ball out of tall grass.

There were local rules for golf games in Henderson County back in 1906. A ball driven out of bounds could be dropped on the fair green with the loss of one stroke. A ball falling near a tree or fence could be moved two club lengths without penalty but not nearer to the green. And remember that cattle grazing on the green took the place of a mowing machine. A ball falling in a cow track, a ditch or a marsh could be lifted and dropped over the shoulder with the loss of only one stroke.

And for many years, between golf games, Captain Smyth's flock of sheep kept the grass on his hillside neatly trimmed while creating a pastoral scene that slowed many a motorist traveling down Little River Road.

Kingdom of the Happy Land

A weathered stone chimney still stands on the North Carolina/South Carolina state line a few miles south of Flat Rock. Several pits that once served as cellars are beds of weeds and uncut grass now, and only the chimney is left to suggest you're driving through history. Yet you're where a band of emancipated slaves found a new life in what they called their Kingdom of the Happy Land.

Where had they come from? Where did they expect their journey to lead them? Having spent their lives in bondage, they welcomed freedom, but few expected the complications that would result from being forced to leave the plantations that had harbored them for several generations. Yet they began a journey that would lead them through Alabama, Georgia and South Carolina. On their way, other families joined them, and fortunately they were able to follow the leadership of a man who was one of the few among his race who had been given an education. Religious matters, too, had played an important role in his upbringing and would continue to dominate his life.

It is impossible for us, in the comfort of our homes, to imagine the hardships of such a journey undertaken by people who had no means of transportation and no way of knowing how many exhausting miles they would have to walk before they could find a safe place for a night's rest. But when the band of travelers reached South Carolina and learned of the migration each summer from Charleston to Flat Rock, they learned, too, of properties in some cases amounting to hundreds of acres. They wondered if some of their group might find work on those farmlands.

So they pushed on, at last reaching North Carolina and the vast acreage of Oakland, the home of Colonel John Davis's widow and her son. There they were given permission to stay, working for people in the area and caring for animals on the farms. The Davises gave them land to build their houses, where they could follow the lifestyle of their forebears. Their able leader, referred to by them as their king, was Robert Montgomery, who had taken the surname of the man in whose house he had grown up. Since Robert was unmarried, his brother's wife, Louella, was the queen, and their "palaces" faced each other from opposite sides of the state line.

The kingdom was established after the Civil War, and it continued into the early 1900s. Members worked in various positions in Flat Rock and Hendersonville and for a time lived in the area when the kingdom was no longer a homeland. One of the women had a small house on Little River Road and was a familiar sight driving her pony cart to various houses to pick up the laundry she did for the residents.

When the kingdom disbanded, a small piece of land across the road from Flat Rock's Teneriffe was given to one of the women who had worked for Flat Rock people. She had a cabin built and lived there until she was nearly one hundred. The cabin is gone now. For a time, the site of it was a small graveyard for servants of Teneriffe. Then the property changed hands, and with time, history gave way to the present. A modern house now stands over the graves of a once highly respected black family.

Ask people nowadays to tell you about the Kingdom of the Happy Land. Only someone who lived near the edge of it knows the real story.

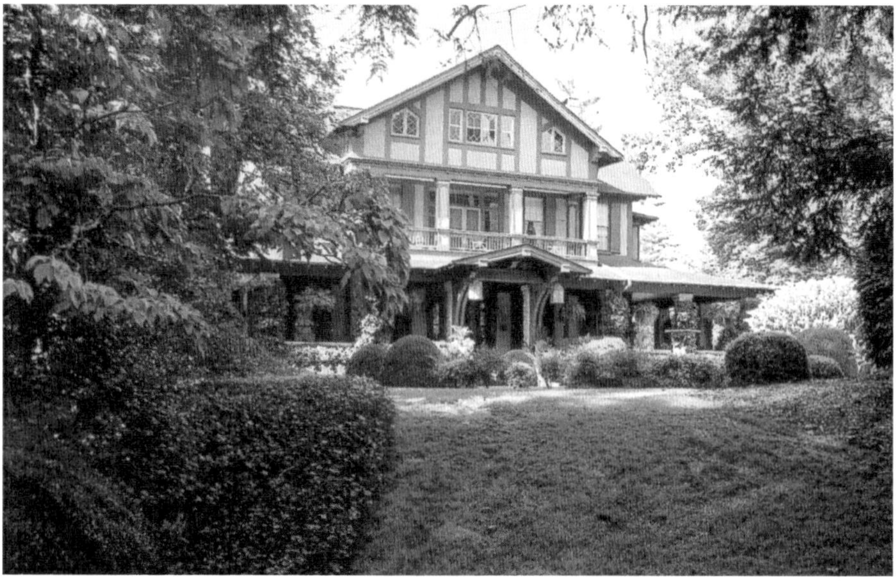

The stately home named Teneriffe at Flat Rock. *Photo by Terry Ruscin with permission of Helen and Marvin Seibold.*

Looking for Napoleons

Climb to the top of Glassy Mountain and look toward the west, the opposite side of the mountain from where Roger Richardson Hill's stone mausoleum has stood now since 1927. If you find someone up there with a mattock (or perhaps you call it a pickaxe) digging into the rocky soil, he may not be anxious to tell you why he's doing it. He'll finally let on, though, that he's hoping to find some napoleons. You're noticeably surprised if you, like most of us, are familiar with the toothsome dessert by that name, and you know good and well you don't dig for that. Then it occurs to you that you've read about those French princes who kept the name of their great countryman Napoleon prominent throughout former centuries. You might wonder if some careless scribe just failed to capitalize the "n" when writing about those princes.

The napoleon I'm referring to doesn't qualify for capitalization due to the particular way in which it's involved with a person. According to my unabridged dictionary, a lower-case-"n" napoleon is "a former gold coin of France equal to 20 francs and bearing a portrait of either Napoleon I or III." But if the diggers should find any of those coins on Glassy, how in the world did they get there? And anyone who wonders why Napoleon II doesn't appear on any of the coins must bear in mind that he, the son of Napoleon I and father of Napoleon III, came into prominence after the Battle of Waterloo, but only for a brief time, for he died of tuberculosis when still a young man.

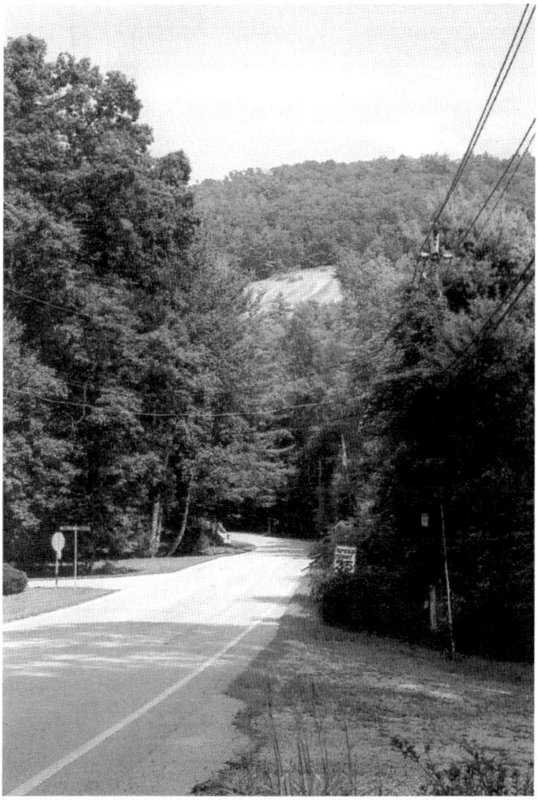

A view of Glassy Mountain from Little River Road. *Photo by Terry Ruscin.*

We know from the history books that back in the 1500s,

Hernando de Soto passed near what is now Hendersonville. France and Spain had already come close to waging war when both countries wanted access to, and were willing to fight for, the sassafras plants growing abundantly in the Blue Ridge Mountains and providing highly valued medications for a variety of ailments. Could de Soto have brought the napoleons?

We read that gold was dug from our foothills a long time before its true value was known. As cheap and readily available as the metal was, one family even found a large lump of it highly satisfactory for a doorstop before the owner had a chance to sell the lump for $3.50, which was said to be a good price at the time.

While it's doubtful anyone digging on Glassy Mountain nowadays expects to find gold, the efforts might still be rewarding, for we know there were a few isolated families living at the top of the mountain when the Civil War was going on, and a handful remained until present times. Some of them, fearing being robbed, dug into the clay to bury valuable items on our mountains. Not many years ago I was shown where a short trench had been dug several feet into a clay bank bordering a seldom-traveled road. Silver and gold pieces had been put into the trench and then the opening was filled back up with the clay, keeping the items safe until the war was history.

Could the diggers recently seen on Glassy be a later generation of people who had heard it told that their forebears brought napoleons with them for financial support when they came nearby with de Soto? Were the diggers looking for napoleons?

It does seem odd, though, that a gold coin, a tasty delicacy and a prince of France, none having anything in common with the others, should bear the same name.

ICEHOUSES

A few icehouses still stand on Flat Rock properties, although for uses far different from those for which they were built. They still provide space for storage, but not for storing ice, which had been their original purpose. Refrigeration has played a major role in doing away with them as a necessity, and changes occurring in weather patterns over the years have had a significant effect on them. Our old-timers will vouch for that, stoutly maintaining, as they do, that winters are not as cold as they used to be.

Built of stone or concrete, the icehouse stood behind the main house. In winter, when ice was deep on neighborhood ponds, men cut out great chunks of it and stored them inside the icehouses between layers of pine needles or sawdust. At one country home, evidence still stands as proof of a seven-foot rock-lined pit with a dirt floor to allow drainage and a structure at the top to provide protection, ensuring storage of ice for the family occupying the house as long ago as 1900.

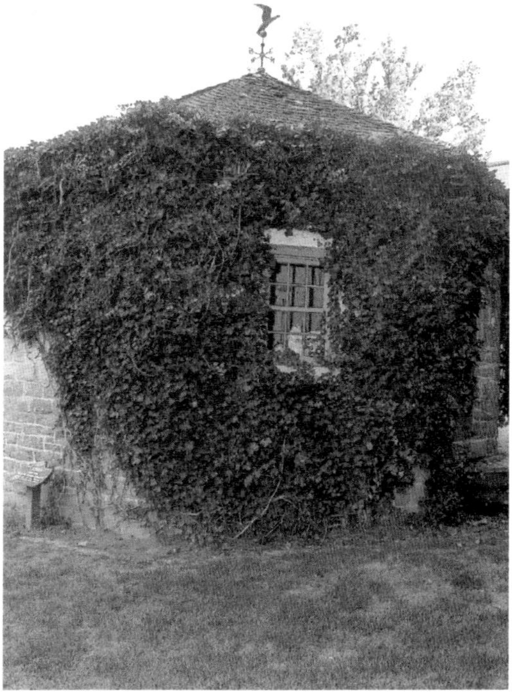

The potting shed/wash house—originally an icehouse and then a cistern—at Teneriffe, Flat Rock. *Photo by Terry Ruscin with permission of Helen and Marvin Seibold.*

A member of Connemara's Smyth family remembered that, as a little boy spending time with his grandfather at Connemara, he saw the hired men cut ice from the shallow pond that is still seen by travelers on Little River Road. He said the men made rough sleds out of sourwood poles eight inches through and turned up at the ends. When they'd sawed through the ice and worked the chunks of it out with pry poles, they hauled it on the makeshift sleds to the icehouse and put it through the trapdoor, the only opening at the top of the structure built over the icehouse. Thus protected from sun and warming rains, the ice lasted throughout most of the year.

When summer temperatures brought people out of the torrid flatlands into the refreshing mountain air, the old-time hand-cranked ice cream churns were brought into the kitchens for use. Custard made with thick cream and fresh eggs and sugar was cooked and chilled and poured into a metal container inside the churn. Rock salt was added to the ice to slow its melting, added ever so carefully so that none of it accidentally fell into the container. Then eager people took turns with the handle until the custard stiffened and was finally ready to be scooped out and eaten. It was little wonder that the ice-cream churn was a legend in southern living.

There was already ice on the neighborhood ponds at a particular time when temperatures suddenly dropped still lower. Nowadays it seems unbelievable,

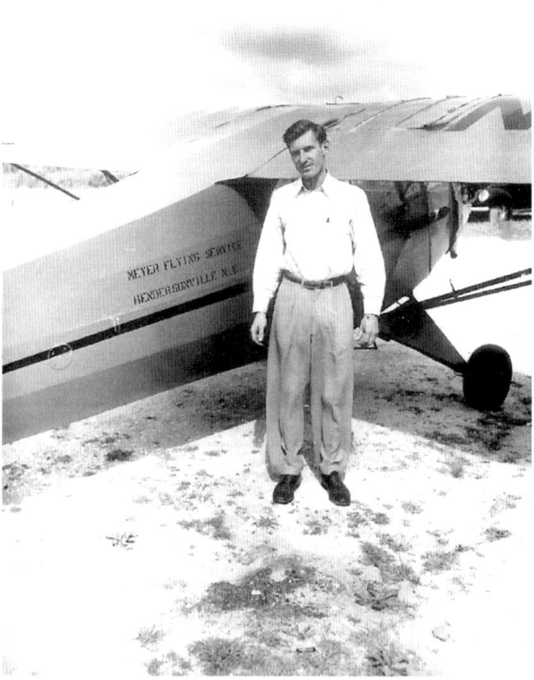

Oscar Meyer and his airplane. *Photo courtesy of John Paul Jones.*

but to prove how thick the ice was on Wolf Lake [between Crab Creek Road and Little River Road], a man drove his car onto it just to prove it was solid enough to support so much weight. And young Oscar Meyer, who had made his first airplane, landed it on a frozen section of Highland Lake. Holding onto a long rope attached to the tail of the plane, a group of young folks wearing ice skates zigzagged across the glassy surface.

Now and then the young folks took chances, like a time a couple of boys were sliding on the frozen lake in front of Captain Smyth's Connemara. The ice gave way under one of the boys, but thankfully his companion was close enough to him to grab him by his hair and keep him from sinking full length into the frigid water.

Icehouses are virtually forgotten now, and if our winters continue to get warmer a particular way of life will be history.

The Moonshine Still Next Door

It's said that not many years ago coyotes made their way "from off" into our environment. I don't know just when it was, but they were here when my husband Joe was delivering an appreciable number of Henderson County's new citizens. With as little sleep as seemed adequate for him, he was able to keep going through long days, as well as being constantly interrupted at night, but he could always reach the delivery room at the hospital without speeding dangerously from home just in the nick of time. That's how it was on a night that keeps coming to mind.

By two o'clock in the morning, his job at the delivery room was done, and he headed home hoping he would be able to sleep until morning. He turned into our half-mile dirt driveway—and a high-pitched scream totally unfamiliar to him broke the stillness of the woods between our driveway and the property next door. Beginning low and then raising several notes higher, it penetrated the darkness, convincing Joe beyond any possible doubt that it had come from a woman in dire distress. He floorboarded the accelerator as he bumped on home and dashed in to telephone the sheriff. Then he paced the porch floor until the sheriff and his deputy slammed to a stop in our yard. They hurried to where the sound had been, pausing first to pick up a neighbor, who, without a moment's hesitation, called the whole idea absurd.

No one, no vehicle, was in sight on that abandoned road between the neighbor's house and ours. No evidence of any kind hinted that anyone had been near. So the sheriff and his deputy returned to headquarters to wait for more information to reach them, if any happened to be offered.

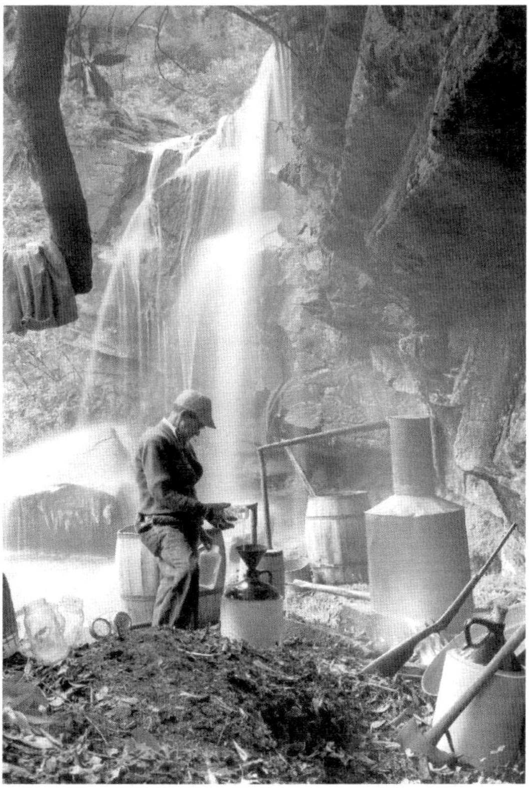

A moonshiner tends his still. *Photo courtesy of the Henderson County Genealogical and Historical Society, Inc.*

A few days later, the sheriff returned to the premises, and that was when he found out what had been going on. A moonshine still had been constructed between the high banks bordering the road between us and our neighbor, smack in the middle of that red-clay road that joined the one that was hardly ever traveled anymore except at times throughout the summer season.

Since the arrangement was about as handy for the neighbor as he needed it to be, as well as the fact that only some of his customers walked, he had those particular ones leave their cars just off the main road when they patronized his business. Their purpose being what it was, the ones who were more accustomed to walking than they were to riding had no objection to continuing on foot.

When you hear about them, though, you wonder what would happen nowadays if a man were slinking through the woods with a jug of moonshine over his shoulder and a pack of coyotes he'd never heard before echoing along his path. It's not unlikely his habits would become instant history.

Names of Mountains

As beautiful as our drives around the countryside are, they're even more appealing if we know the names of the mountains surrounding us. Some of those names remind us of the early settlers who moved into the area when land grants were given in return for commendable service during the Revolutionary War; others came later when word spread through the Lowcountry of South Carolina that the cooler temperatures we enjoy on summer nights would restore good health, especially to people plagued with malaria.

Our mountains have been known by name longer than any of us here now can say, and only if we climb to the tops of some of them can we understand why they bear the particular names they do. Others, like Forge Mountain, for example, let people a long time ago know that valuable metals could be found in our mountain soil by anyone wanting to dig for them.

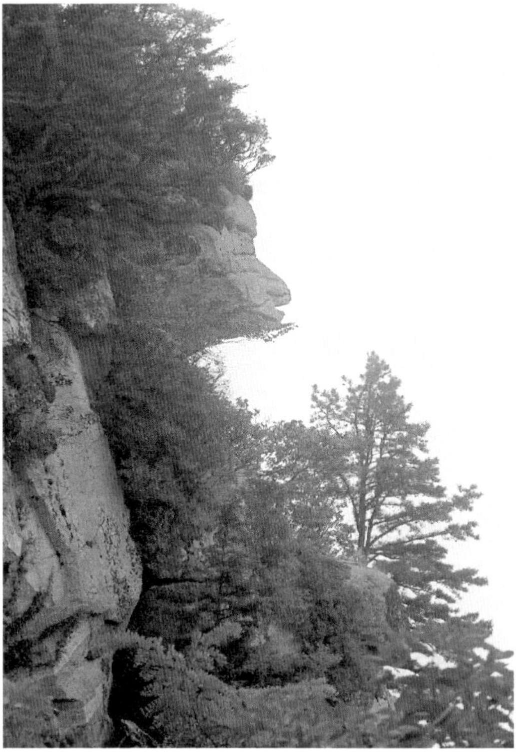

Caesars Head, a granite-gneiss outcropping atop the Blue Ridge escarpment in Greenville County, South Carolina. This formation in Caesars Head State Park was formed approximately 409 million years ago and stands 3,266 feet above sea level. *Photo by Terry Ruscin.*

Caesars Head south of Brevard has long been a delight of sightseers willing and able to take the steep walk down a path leading to the best view of the stone profile of "Caesar," who seems to be looking over the vast territory he might have conquered. There's no sugar on Sugar Loaf Mountain, but bears are undoubtedly in abundance on Bear Wallow.

But what about Pinnacle?

We know a pinnacle is a topmost point, and we have no trouble seeing Pinnacle Mountain when we drive out Crab Creek Road or head south on the Greenville Highway, or from various other places in the county, but nowhere on that mountain do we see a highest point—a pinnacle. The mountain has the shape of a loaf of bread. The road across the top is fairly level, but at one place that shuts out the public now with a high fence and a locked gate, tremendous boulders stand on the edge of a precipice. The fence hasn't always been there, and hikers used to climb onto the highest boulder to have their pictures taken. Because of those boulders, the mountain was originally known as Pinnacle Rocks.

Venturesome youth have, at times, inspired hikers to shun the road that leads along the face of the mountain and looks out over Crab Creek Valley. They believed shortcuts were much quicker, though infinitely steeper. When college classmates visited at my house, I took them to the top of Pinnacle to see the sunrise, a new experience for most of them since they were nearly all from the flatlands of South Carolina, our college being Winthrop, the South Carolina College for Women.

Near the top of the mountain, we walked past the home of Elzie Floyd, the blind man who walked alone to town and anywhere else he wanted to go. He could tell you the name of whatever knoll he was crossing, although he had never been able to see the trails he followed across "Tater Hill." Then he stopped in the community of "Cat Head" to pass the time of day with friends. Elzie said he could tell by the way his feet felt on the path he was walking whether he was on the one leading to where he wanted to go.

Nowadays, a good road climbs past Cat Head and levels off at the site where Elzie's house once stood. Then it drops down the western edge of Pinnacle. The drive across it will be spectacular when the autumn leaves have turned. If you take it, though, be sure to have a map with you so you can identify the mountains you may not have realized were there.

A Pioneer Way of Life

Pinnacle Mountain

Riding along a well-maintained road across Pinnacle Mountain recently brought to mind thoughts of my first trip to the topmost rocks to see the breathtaking view from east to west and on out to Mills River Valley, the other side of Hendersonville. I had walked up the mountain many times, but only once had I gone in a wagon pulled by two mules as I had done the first time I had been taken there.

Many times later, on foot I scurried up shortcuts between levels of the narrow wagon road where trails had been cut and were steep enough to make me pause often to catch my breath. The higher I climbed, the more rewarding was the view of Pisgah, the Rat to one side of it, Long John and others clearly visible against the horizon.

Once when I was a child, my dad took his family on a camping trip, driving his automobile first to the Stepps' house on Pinnacle. There, Mary Stepp's brother, Bub, hitched his mules to a wagon and drove us along rocky ruts to where he had hacked out a campsite for us. We had no tents. For my sister and me, heavy lap robes were opened on the ground just under the wagon bed in case a sudden shower should come. Our cousin "Peg," who was always her happiest when she was out of doors, rolled up in a lap robe under the stars. Mary and her brother and sister were near us, but no other campers were within miles, nor were any houses, except one that amounted to a single room. I remember the ingenuity of those isolated people who lived there and found frugal ways to make do, such as shutting out wind that otherwise would have blown between ill-fitting boards in the walls. Those

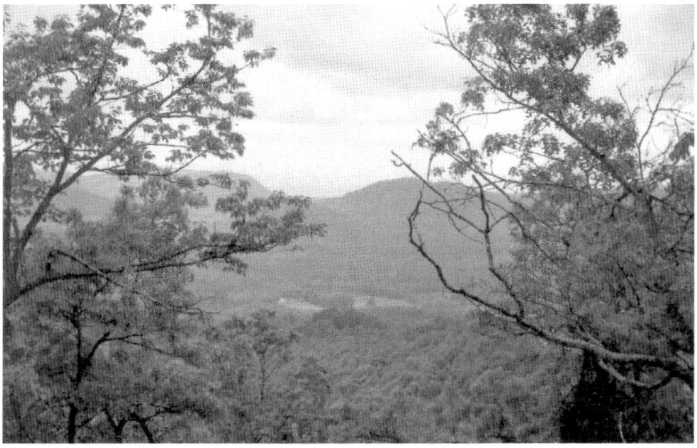

A view from Pinnacle Mountain. *Photo by Terry Ruscin.*

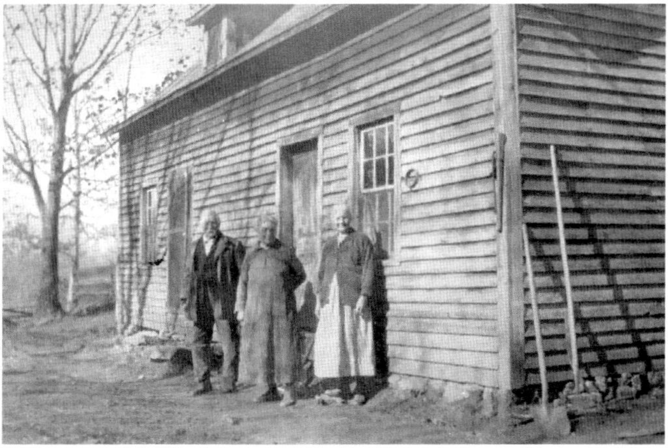

The Stepp family and their cabin on Pinnacle Mountain. Pictured from left to right: "Bub," Mary and Ellen. *Photo courtesy of Joseph Bailey Jr.*

people had lined the inside of the little house with old newspapers. Whether anyone in the family could read, I never knew, but the one-room schoolhouse was nowhere near, and what really mattered was warmth when mountain winters came.

You don't hear now of mountain boomers, but we ate them on those camping trips. They're close kin to squirrels, but somewhat smaller, and they're mighty tasty when cooked over the campfire you're sitting by when you've come down trails that seemed close to being straight up and down. Webster's unabridged dictionary doesn't even list mountain boomers, and people just look at me quizzically when I mention them and ask if anyone can tell me something about them. I can only suppose the name must have been purely local.

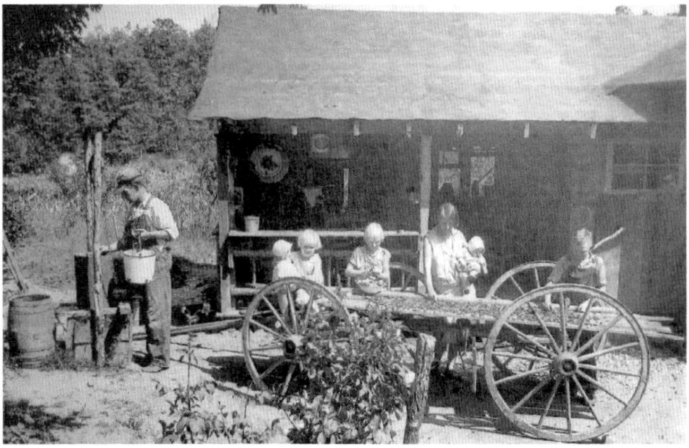

A typical pioneer family, circa 1900. *Photo courtesy of the Henderson County Genealogical and Historical Society, Inc.*

I confess to often overlooking the fact that many people never knew Mary and her brother and sister on Pinnacle Mountain, never having camped in a vast wilderness the public had never visited. But my recollections of experiences we had there were all the more unconventional, and more intriguing, because of the nature of it.

Never mind the crushed rock stretches and paved double lanes winding along the mountain roads we were traveling just recently. Distant views were magnificent, and modern red brick houses were all along the roadsides. I'll just go on harboring recollections of those camping trips we took a very long time ago and of daybreak hikes to the top of Pinnacle Mountain to watch the sun rise—even if we arrived on the high rocks before an early morning haze had lifted.

The Stepps on Pinnacle

Little remains of an old homeplace at the base of Pinnacle Mountain. You could look up from the yard and see giant boulders on one edge of the mountain's crest, and if you climbed up there and balanced yourself on top of one of the boulders, you could see almost to Asheville. Along the mountainside, a road, cut long ago so wagons could haul timber out to a sawmill, still snakes its way through the forest. A trail used to provide shortcuts between the road's switchbacks, cutting the walking distance, but it was almost straight up and down.

My friend James tells me about his great-grandmother having been born and brought up at the foot of Pinnacle. In later years, his great-uncle built a frame house out of poplar lumber sawed from trees growing on his property. But James says he has never understood why, when his great-uncle's family owned considerable acreage, the log cabin, and later the frame house, were built as far as they were from the creek that supplied water for the family and their livestock. He said his great-uncle, even as an old man, led his two mules a quarter of a mile and back twice a day to drink from a small stream flowing out of a spring on one side of the mountain. The family's drinking water was carried in pails from a different spring, one a hundred feet below the "new house," as the family continued to call the one that had replaced the old log cabin.

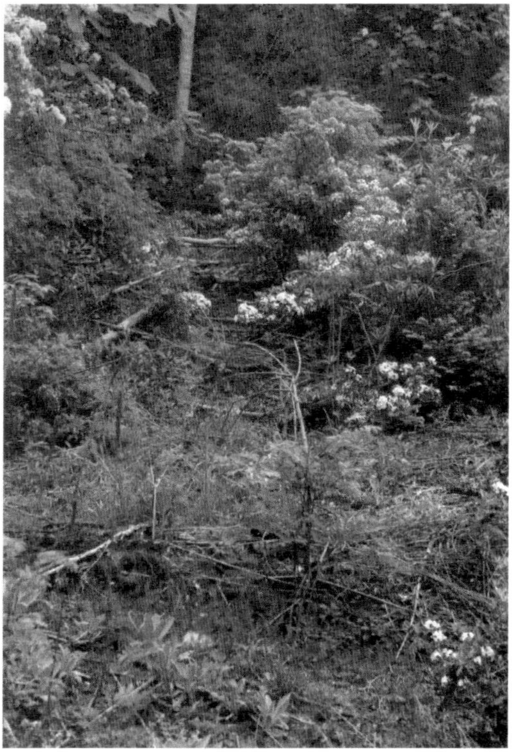

The overgrown trailhead to the Stepp cabin on Pinnacle Mountain. *Photo by Terry Ruscin.*

James spoke of one of his great-aunts. He said she had married and moved to an area on Pinnacle called Dark Cove because fogs that rose over the waters of Green River in the early mornings were thick enough to shut out the sunshine for hours along the five-mile stretch between the river and the house.

The trail was rough. Roots and rocks were underfoot, and tangled vines grew along the edges. Yet during the Civil War, James's great-grandmother, Fanny Stepp [mother of Mary, Bub and Ellen], followed the trail at night, her only light a torch made of rich pine shoots and set afire. She went from her house at the foot of Pinnacle to the headwaters of Green River to warn a kinsman living there that Confederates were in the area looking for men who were hiding out in the mountains, refusing to join the army.

James has treasured memories of his great-uncle, who, he says, "brought history to life when he rebuilt wagon wheels by the old way of heating the iron rims and shrinking them to fit the wheels." He shot wild turkeys with a muzzleloading rifle made by the Gillespie family on Mills River, and he sold twenty-pound turkeys for one dollar apiece.

When James pays today's price for a pint jar of honey, he remembers when a large chestnut tree was cut down in order to hive a swarm of bees. He said the men removed enough honey to fill two large washtubs.

The old homeplace on the lower edge of Pinnacle Mountain now belongs to DuPont, and its Friends Association is eager to preserve its history. I wish they could have visited the people who lived in the "new house" from the time of the Civil War until the mid-1900s. They would have stayed for dinner, for without prearranged plans the Stepp women had a meal ready for anyone who climbed the mountain. "Hit ain't much, but if ye can put up with poor folks' rations yer welcome to it" would have been the simple and sincere invitation to a meal that covered two yards of bright, red-checked oilcloth with dishes of country ham and fried chicken, homegrown vegetables, biscuits and corn pone.

Only a stone chimney is left now. But a good road follows the top of the ridge, and when you get to the boulders you can look down and see where the "new house" stood for nearly one hundred years.

Mary

Forget Mary? Never. I can still remember when she came to our house to look after my sister, Jennie, and me when we were not yet of school age. Mary rode on the bare plank that served as a wagon seat, and her brother, Bub, drove the white mule John and the black one Bill. Bub reined in the mules beside our house, and Mary stepped down. She followed us into the parlor, as living rooms were called then, and when Grandma offered her a chair, Mary chose the straightest one and sat with her feet slightly apart and motionless, her thumbs circling one another on her lap. After she and Grandma had talked for a little while, she said to Jennie and me, "C'mon. Le's y'ns and me go out in the woods and build ye a playhouse." From that moment, she was our friend.

Whether sewing for us on a treadle machine or walking with us in town to pass the time of day with her kinfolks coming in to buy sugar and flour, she ever kept us near her and as properly behaved as possible.

When evenings came at our house and her day's work was done, Mary eased the door between the hall and the living room slightly open and looked in quietly. She waited until my father saw her and asked her to sit with us, and then she talked of her life on Pinnacle Mountain. Although a very young child at the time, I was struck with her memories, but I didn't know how much I was learning firsthand about pioneer times from one who had lived them.

And when I spent time with Mary's sister and brother, I saw how they lived, whether working at the usual regimens of independent country life or resting by an oak log fire at evening times.

Ellen refrigerated milk and butter in a springhouse at the foot of the hill, and I may sometimes have counted how many trips she made to bring back what she needed for the meal ahead. I learned how she had taken shortcuts when she walked the seven miles from her house to town because the jolting of the wagon hurt her back. I saw old-time ways. And I remember Bub resting in sunshine pouring in through his open front door with no screen to block it while he rolled his cigarette from the pack of cigarette papers and a small bag of tobacco he kept in his pocket.

A rough road rarely traveled by automobiles led to the four-room clapboard house on a shelf above Dismal Creek. Two large, square slabs of granite—the front steps—one loosely placed on top of the other, lay at the front door, and a red-clay bank stood behind the house. In the main room downstairs were two beds, one with a deep feather mattress and the other—Bub's bed—with a corn shuck that rustled with his slightest move. Underneath the feather bed a hole some six or seven inches wide had been cut to allow cats to come and go without the door having to be opened for them.

A crude staircase led to Ellen's bedroom, and just past the stairs, Jennie and I shared a bed next to Mary's. I remember the feather mattress Jennie warned me not ever to crawl over, even at the foot, so I wouldn't squash the feathers on her side; my alternative was the unappealing task of crawling underneath the entire bed in order to squeeze between it and the angle where the sloping roof joined the wall. Crawling underneath the bed, over and around whatever was stored there, I'd find my way in the faint, flickering light of a kerosene lamp. There was too little space to squirm between the bed and the roof on my side.

Yet I know now that while those times at Pinnacle were in vivid contrast to the ways of my coastal relatives who regularly occupied their summer homes in Flat Rock and looked to employees to see to the work, it was a special privilege for me to have been where I often was when I was growing up.

As time went by and friends at school were buying new dancing slippers, I was often walking the two-mile clay wagon road from the Old CCC Road to turn at the bars that kept Ellen's cows close by. Whether my dad drove us to where he could turn the car around or whether we walked depended on the weather. Mary always carried what she called the "Pinnacle grip," a large cloth sack containing our clothes, which she could wash when necessary in a black iron pot beside Dismal Creek and hang on surrounding bushes to dry.

With no way to let Ellen and Bub know we were coming, we just showed up, no matter how long we planned to stay. Ellen never failed to say she "lowed we'd be a-comin'" about then, and as isolated as she was, no telephone being within five miles of her, I wondered if it might have been wishful thinking.

At mealtimes, Bub took his place at one end of the table, and Mary and Ellen made sure his needs were satisfied. When they were, he poured his coffee to "saucer and blow" before he drank it.

When my family attended my college graduation, Mary came with them. As I showed her portraits of dignitaries in their academic attire, she told me proudly, "Now when you graduate I want a picture of you in your shroud."

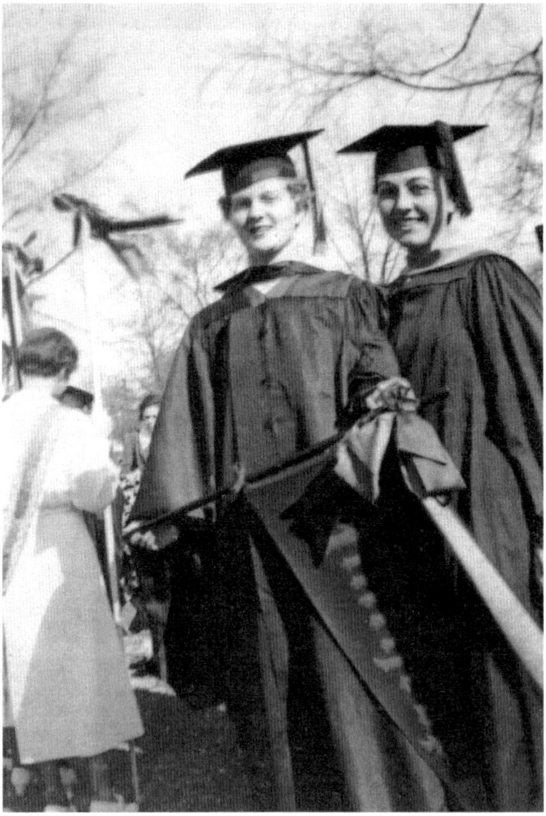

Louise Howe's graduation ceremony at Winthrop College, Rock Hill, South Carolina, 1936. *Photo courtesy of Joseph Bailey Jr.*

Mary spent her last years in her old home on Pinnacle Mountain, content with the lifestyle she had known as a child when the Civil War was attempting to settle problems between North and South but made little difference to people in isolated mountain cabins.

My thanks go to Mary, to the chance for those Pinnacle trips with my dad, when he made house calls to patients in the far corners of the county, and to having been able to appreciate such individuals as, for example, the woman who came to the door of my husband's office holding one hand in the air and announcing vehemently that she had reached down to give the dog a dead rat. “But,” she said, “he got a-holt o’ my finger instead, and I’ve come to git me a technical shot.”

I have known little related to dullness even on the most dismal days.

Bub

I did a good thing when I had a carport built outside my bedroom window. Not necessarily with the care of the car in mind but because raindrops splashing on the metal roof of the structure make a delightful sound as I fall asleep. It takes me back to childhood visits to friends whose pioneer way of life on Pinnacle Mountain is history now, but I realize what a privilege it was for me to know the people living it.

The red-clay yard was our playground. Neither whirligig nor metal slide, but there was a small mound of red clay. Unless you’ve done it, you can’t imagine what fun it was to stand barefooted on such a mound after a summer shower and wriggle your toes enough to inch you over to the edge of it. There our feet could lose their grip and send us skidding to level ground. We had to be careful not to let our feet slip out from under us, for muddy clothing was hard to come clean, even on the old scrub board and in suds from a cake of homemade lye soap.

Waking up early on Pinnacle was easy. There was the call bringing cows to the milking shed, and hens cackled. Home-cured bacon sizzled in a black iron frying pan, and a pan of ice-cold spring water waited in the kitchen to wash sleepiness away. My sister was always downstairs ahead of me, so I could roll across her side of the bed instead of crawling underneath it.

Unless you’ve tried it, you can’t imagine how difficult it is to keep your balance on the sloping side of a haystack. But that made climbing it all the more fun. What it did to Bub Stepp’s efforts to preserve his hay was a pitiable sight, to say the least, and that was what he saw when he went by the stacks on his way to take his mules to the creek for a drink of water. He was the one with his haystacks to rebuild, but my sister and I would remember what fun we’d had trying to climb up the side of that loosely piled hay.

Driving through the countryside nowadays, we no longer see what used to be one of the most familiar sights by midsummer. There was a time we saw fodder stacks drying in abandoned cornfields. Now, landscaped lawns and decorative plantings border the roadways, and we admire the handiwork of the people who spread such beauty for others, as well as themselves, to enjoy. But for us who grew up in the country, something is definitely missing.

We used to see haystacks dotting the landscape. We know there's still plenty of hay being grown, but now it's cut in long, wide strips and rolled into bales, and although it may be easier to handle that way, bales are by no means as picturesque as the old-time haystacks that stood taller than the barn beside them. Nor do hay bales bring back memories to those of us who used to try to climb the hay, long a delight in the lives of young folks growing up in the country, just as it was when my sister and I were growing up and often visited Ellen Stepp and her brother, Bub, on Pinnacle Mountain.

I can still see Bub with his pitchfork, tossing hay onto a pile that began in a big circle at his feet and ended half again as tall as he was and pointed at the top. The stacks stood near the barn, along with half a dozen or so apple trees that had borne fruit since his mother planted them soon after the Civil War. There were several varieties: "rusty coats," Ellen called the little brown-skinned sweet apples; "horse" apples, she called the tart green ones that grew so big she needed only one to fill a pie crust.

One day my sister climbed one haystack as far up as the hay supported her. I climbed another. Each of us had our pockets full of big green "horse" apples and the bombardment began. Our intention was not to hit each other but to come alarmingly close to it. Success piqued our excitement—and alerted Bub, who brought an abrupt end to our "battle" before one of us could inadvertently damage the other.

The neatly rolled bales we see nowadays are unquestionably a mark of progress. But an old-time haystack beside a weathered barn would bring back memories of days long past. It's too bad we never see them anymore. And young folks growing up in these modern days of landscaped lawns and picturesque plantings are missing a lot of fun that came with old-time country living.

Remembering Names

It's always nice to run into someone who seems genuinely glad to see you even if you haven't the faintest idea who the person is. Perhaps a law should be passed requiring people to identify themselves even before they set in on the "How y'alls" and other platitudes. Of course, there are those fortunate individuals who never forget a name, but I'm not one of them. There are others who remember faces, but I regretfully have to admit I'm not one of them either. I just have to wait for something in the conversation to clue me in on recognition, and that was what happened recently when I was in that very situation. The man greeted me in a friendly manner, and then said, "You don't know who I am, do you?" I had to confess I didn't. Embarrassing, yes, but better than his thinking me downright rude. Then he mentioned the name of his in-laws. "You can take it from there," he said, and he was right. I could name just about all of five generations of them.

During our conversation, one of us mentioned an old-timer known to friends, as well as to kin, as "Uncle Bubby." The fellow said he was just a boy when Uncle Bubby died, but he remembered the mules that pulled his wagon to town and back every Saturday. I remembered those mules too, a black one named Bill and a white one named John. There were times I rode in the wagon with Uncle Bubby to visit the two sisters he lived with on Pinnacle Mountain.

"We bought John when Uncle Bubby died," the fellow told me. Then our conversation ended, and he went on to attend to the business he'd come to town to see to, and I went on with what I had to do. But I went with memories of more than three-quarters of a century ago, when a particular lifestyle was still going on in the four corners of Henderson County, and I had the privilege of knowing people who lived it.

I thought about it during our recent cold snap when we were putting on our warmest clothing, pushing up our thermostats and turning on the heaters in our automobiles. I remembered Uncle Bubby sitting on that cold plank he used for a wagon seat, his jacket open to wind and rain. A few canvas-covered wagons were still in use, but he preferred not to shut out familiar sights along the miles between home and town. He was never seen in an overcoat, although one hung on the wall of his house on the mountain. He was saving it, he said, for when he might need it, but whatever specific occasion he had in mind, he never said. The coat hung on a nail where he had put it the day it was given to him by a family friend. No matter how much Uncle Bubby was out in the worst of weather, he never wore the coat.

Many years ago, when it was customary for people across the county to come to town on Saturdays, cold winter days found them clustered in sunny spots on the sidewalks discussing matters of interest to them. One man, besides never wearing an overcoat, didn't button his shirt all the way to the top, no matter what the temperature was.

We don't want to go back to times of smoking fireplaces and a woodpile that needs constant replenishing. We'll take our cars with push-button heaters and our houses with tempering radiators.

And we'll hope to keep on running into people who claim us as friends.

ELLEN

When Jim Perry called Ellen Stepp "the aristocrat of the mountains," he was right. No one who knew her would have had the slightest doubt of it.

Throughout her life of more than ninety years, Ellen belonged to Pinnacle Mountain. Since getting to and from the schoolhouse would have meant walking a couple of miles each way, even as a little child, and education not being compulsory then, she never learned to read or even to write her name. Many years later, when she was advised to make a will for when one would become necessary, she objected adamantly, insisting her sister was "the onliest person" to get the meager savings that would be available right where she was stashing them for safekeeping among the rafters when she was paid by customers for home-churned butter and freshly dressed fryers. Wrapping the savings in old newspapers, she had secreted them entirely to her satisfaction.

When her sister died, Ellen, the sole heir, was obliged to talk to an attorney, although she didn't really see why and made him quite aware of it. He tried to explain, patiently at first but more firmly as he went along, and realized that the honor of his profession was not entirely clear in Ellen's mind. He persisted, though, until at last he convinced Ellen that she must sign the necessary paper concerning her inheritance. When she did, though, with her hand guided by his, she made only an X accompanying the name he had written where her signature belonged. She had never had a reason to learn to write it.

Although spending her life on Pinnacle Mountain, caring for herself and her chickens and her cow and never reading or writing, Ellen lived independently. Her home was a stopping place for hikers climbing the mountain, and whether they knew her or not, they looked down from Pinnacle Rocks to the gray clapboard house and called to Ellen to ask her to have a meal ready for them when they came by. Ellen always obliged them, promptly stirring the fire in her kitchen stove and waylaying a chicken or two in the yard. New friends were made, and many hikers remembered her in thoughtful ways.

Many visitors wrote down their home addresses, and at Christmastime Ellen walked the two-mile road to a neighbor's house to have the armloads of holly and hemlock she "backed" so she could mail them to her friends. She always climbed near the top of the mountain to get what she claimed were the "best grown" greens for them. Many people found time to climb the mountain again and to tell friends back home of the woman living in such remote surroundings that she swept her yard with a homemade broom of rye straws bundled together and secured with twine.

Going to Pinnacle Mountain was a memorable occasion for people who liked to climb the trails to the top of it. Now, no matter what the weather is, they can follow a well-graded road covered with crushed rock and then walk only a short distance to see a breathtaking view across much of Henderson County.

Just be sure you don't take one of the forks leading from that road. There never used to be all of those forks, and when you get to the bottom of one or another of them, you may no longer be in North Carolina.

Ellen, "the aristocrat of the mountains," isn't there to set a place for you at her table, where homegrown servings used to be generous, although she never failed to welcome friend and stranger alike with an apology that "hit ain't much, but if ye can put up with pore folks' rashins, y'uns is welcome to it."

Life at Ellen's House

I've never thought of my path through life as being all that different from ones my contemporaries have trod, but I admit that what I've considered an advantage for me would have seemed a gross disadvantage to many others—like the buckets of water on a shelf in Ellen's kitchen up on Pinnacle Mountain.

The first thing Ellen did every morning was to build a fire in her kitchen stove. Then, with a heavy wooden bucket swinging from each arm, she ignored a narrow trail threading back and forth and went, instead, down a steep bank between her front yard and Dismal Creek. She filled her buckets and climbed back up to set them on the kitchen table. Ladling a dipperful of the water into a small basin and then adding a bit held over from the day before and simmering in a kettle on the stove, she tempered the fresh ice-cold water enough for all of us to wash our faces and hands. When we were done, she threw the suds out the kitchen door, and whatever hen was striding by at that ill-timed moment squawked in protest.

Anyone wanting to quench a thirst during the day drank from the dipper that floated in one of the buckets and then put the dipper back in the water for the next person.

No entertainment was provided for my sister and me on Pinnacle, nor was any necessary, other than a rope swing hanging between two trees and a red-clay mound that made a great slide after summer showers. A hole was cut in the floor of the "front" room, which served as a sitting room but had two beds in it as well in case kinfolks stayed overnight. Cats numbering a dozen or more came and went through the hole. So did winter temperatures when ice coated the trees outside.

I'm glad I didn't worry about it back then, but in later years, I've wondered if rattlesnakes denned underneath the front steps, one laid on top of the other and with ample room for vermin in spaces between. Once a visitor came into the yard to find Ellen's brother, Uncle Bubby, asleep in a straight chair out in the sunshine. A coiled rattler was within easy reach of him. If alarmed, the snake would strike, but fortunately a hoe was leaning against the house and the visitor's aim was sure.

The nearest telephone was five miles from that house. One day, several of us drove to the bars that kept cows, but not people, out of Ellen's yard. We walked on to the top of Pinnacle. Somewhere along our way the ignition key fell out of my sister's pocket. Although she had already climbed the mountain, she walked to a house halfway to town to telephone our dad to bring us the spare key when he closed his office that evening. Would you believe his office number was just 46?

Spending time with our friends on Pinnacle was a favorite thing to do when my sister and I were growing up, whether for the fun of following Uncle Bubby when he led his mules to drink from a branch of Dismal Creek or just to listen to stories told by people who were keeping pioneer ways alive well into the twentieth century.

Visits on Pinnacle were highlights of my younger years. What an advantage they have afforded me in my desire to write about people whose lives followed paths soon to be forgotten in the fast pace of today.

ELLEN'S DRESSED CHICKENS

It's human nature to develop habits and then to find many of them changing in one way or another as time goes by. We make our daily plans with lifetime customs in mind, whether having a special regard for them or not, but knowing what's likely to happen when certain ones of our ways result from necessity rather than from choice. That's what came to mind the other day as I hurried from the eighty-eight-degree temperature outdoors into the house where the air felt ten degrees cooler than it did outside.

I was thinking about my old friend Ellen, who used to walk from her home on Pinnacle Mountain to Flat Rock and on into town with a large basket hanging from the crook of her arm. She walked in the heat of a burning summer sun and when icicles hung from rock ledges beside her path. It couldn't have been that Ellen enjoyed that arduous walk of close to ten miles in all, but she had no choice. She was obliged to go, for selling her chickens was her means of putting aside money to have when a need of it might arise.

I can see her now as clearly as though it was yesterday. Come Saturday mornings, she filled her basket with dressed fryers, half-pound pats of home-churned butter with a floral design on top and vegetables that had begun ripening in her garden. To us nowadays, the idea of buying a dressed chicken that has not been kept below a certain temperature is unthinkable, yet Ellen had no refrigerator, and only a damp cloth covered the fryers her customers looked forward to buying each week. Even when she sometimes rode with her brother in his wagon, the journey required more time than we can conceive of now, for the mules' steps were slow. But there were times Ellen came to town when her brother didn't.

On those occasions, whether she followed the wagon road across Pinnacle or dropped down through Cat Head to go on out to Crab Creek Road, Ellen had several hours of walking before she reached Flat Rock. From there, Hendersonville was still more than three miles away.

A host of fryers strutted independently through the yard around Ellen's house on Pinnacle. When people who had hiked up the mountain came back down, a chicken dinner was waiting for them, even when the hikers hadn't suggested it, nor had Ellen extended an invitation. Its presence was just her way of making people welcome whether she knew them or not.

If you ever take the Crab Creek Road and turn on the Old CCC Road that follows a crooked route up the lower side of Pinnacle, you'll come to where Ellen's house stood before it was burned by a vagrant seeking shelter in the vacant structure that had been built toward the end of the Civil War. You'll know then what a distance Ellen walked with her basket over her arm, and you'll wonder how people dared eat the fryers when there'd been no way to keep them chilled. Yet no one was ever known to be sick from eating them.

Have we grown unnecessarily cautious nowadays? Possibly, but we have habits now that we prefer to follow, and I daresay one of them will continue to be making the drive from the supermarket to the refrigerator as promptly as we can. We just won't worry about the chicken we've bought if we should happen to have a flat tire on the way home.

Our Natural Heritage

A Ride Through the Woods

It may be rather an odd comparison, but as well aware of the joy I've always had at its completion, I've never spent much time giving more than temporary thought to the brief time waiting, say, for a milkshake to thoroughly serve its purpose. We do live and learn.

"Ready to go?" my son Joe asked me one morning as the front door opened. Because of certain elements of the "going" that I suspected might be involved, a hesitant "Uh" preceded my "Oh yes," knowing that not the least of those elements was the yard-and-a-half-square trailer already hitched to the riding mower and backed against the front steps to enable me to go directly aboard. Taking what I was told was the reserved seat—actually a rather flimsy folding chair with arms—I waited for the perpetrator of the expedition to tie a stout rope to my chair, reach from one side of me to the other and hitch each end of the rope to side boards of the trailer. We were then pronounced ready to go, or rather to take off, which was what was being done, I was told, "in order to get me out of the house for a while." I went in full view of the rocking chairs on my way past the sunny front porch.

I had assumed we would follow the reasonably smooth driveway down to Little River Road and then return home. We didn't do that. We went by way of a footbridge across Pheasant Branch. There we could take a wooded path along the hillside, but we didn't do that either. We skirted the neighbor's fence, rattled and vibrated past a patch of lady's-slippers in full bloom, "turkey foot" [a type of lycopod] and snow-white something-or-other that looked like what's often called lizard's tail [*Saururaceae*], then we skimmed

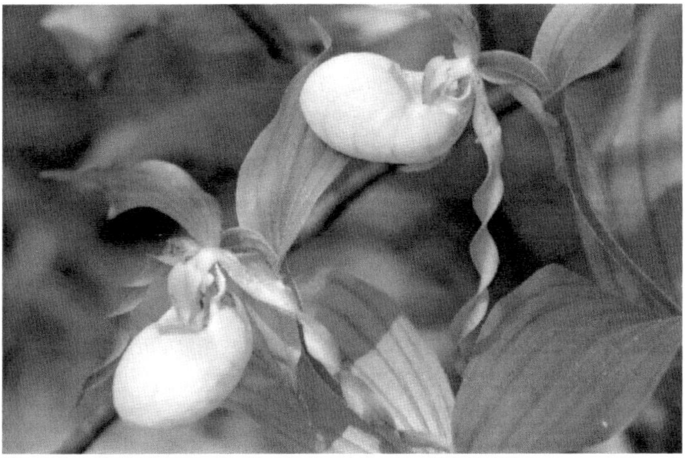

Lady's-slippers.
Photo by Terry Ruscin.

the upper edge of the pond. In a couple of places, both wheels on one side of the trailer weren't even touching the ground. I was thanking providence for the sturdy rope that kept me still onboard, if not in place—however perilously—but at least not dangling.

Talk about a dose of experience!

While in the woods, we followed certain trails that had been what you would call opened if you used the word loosely. I had supposed I wouldn't be seeing those woods again, at least not beyond their edges, for during the past few years I have had no burning desire to come that close to likely running into the coyotes that have moved into our area to live and hunt and howl day or night, but mostly the latter. An old spring is down in there, with water still oozing from a metal spout, and in spite of rampant brush and weeds, there's still a concrete basin that was used long ago for holding items that needed to be kept cool before refrigerators came about.

We have no interest in seeing the coyotes that are down in there. They make enough noise to keep us aware of their whereabouts, and they don't hesitate to walk past us or even close to the house in full daylight. We didn't go near the old spring, though, with the riding mower and the trailer behind it. Anyway, there's not enough room to turn the mower around with the trailer hitched on, no matter how deft the driver is. I don't want to think of his returning to the yard backward. Not with me in the trailer.

I was thinking that, as delightful as it was riding through the woods, there's a lot of difference between sitting in a rocking chair on the porch or spooning a frothy milkshake someone hands you and that bubbly enthusiasm of being taken out of the house for what is called a little spin.

WAITING FOR HUMMINGBIRDS

I know when our hummingbirds come in spring, and I've marked the date on my calendar. I don't know exactly when they leave in autumn, but when I find several days going by without my seeing a hummer dart to and from the container of sugar water I keep providing, there's a change going on. I can't be sure whether the hummers have actually left or whether I'm glancing toward the feeder during one of their temporary absences from it. I've again replenished the supply of sugar water in the feeder on my front porch, though, and right now the hummers seem to be going after it with an eagerness that makes me think they're "tanking up" to begin an imminent flight to Mexico and South America. I marvel at their ability to remember the way, not only there, but also back again to my porch nearly six months later.

With a cupful of sugar water in one hand and the feeder I would pour it into in the other, I was being very careful to avoid spilling any of the liquid on the porch floor where a gathering of big black ants waited for me to miss my mark. To my amazement, a hummer lit on the rim of that feeder I was holding, and he took his time sipping. He was mere inches from my face, which I didn't think was far enough with such a beak as his.

The hummingbirds don't seem to mind my being close to the feeder, although they pause midair right in front of me as if to make sure I'm the one entitled to be there. They take a few sips, and then they disappear for a short while before zooming in on the feeder again. One day, several came at the same time, and their behavior toward one another was by no means courteous. I would not have wanted my hand in the midst of those beaks that are not only long but also sharp.

Hummers are not the only birds well worth the time spent watching them. Think what a pleasure it was for me the day I counted fourteen robins on a grassy plot in my front yard, and all of them were facing the same direction. Some tasty—at least to robins—creatures had apparently just hatched out, because the robins were definitely feasting. At other times, only two or three show up at a time.

What I don't want parading across my front yard is a flock of Canada geese that ignored my premises all summer but evidently remembered a pond at the foot of the hill, and now they're spending entirely too much time there.

A birdfeeder in the yard is a busy spot right now. One visitor has me searching through bird books for his identity, but with the odds against me

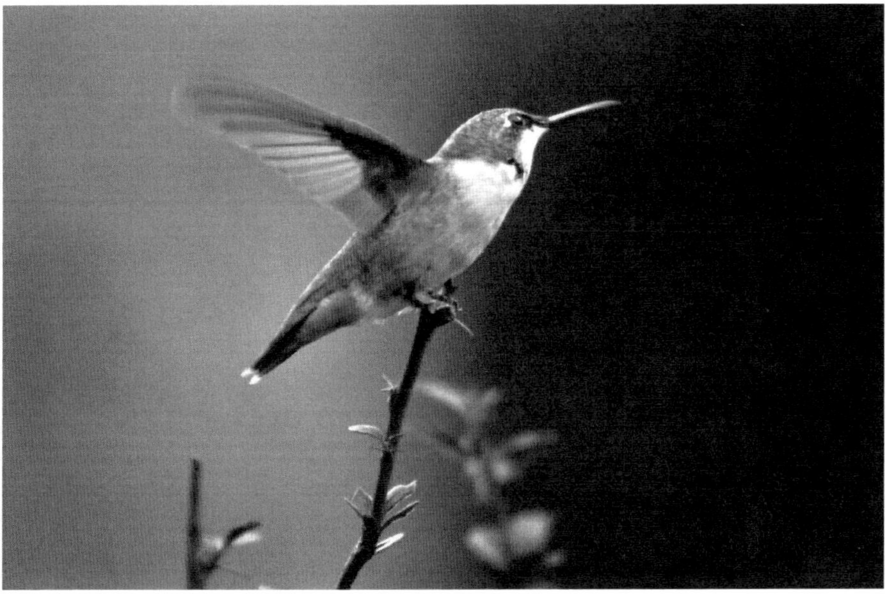

Female ruby-throated hummingbird. *Photo by Terry Ruscin.*

because the feeder is visible through the window beside my favorite chair. The wary bird sees me get out of the chair for a closer look through the binoculars, and the minute I do, he flies out of sight. He's not one of our ordinary birds, but my effort to determine his identity is excuse enough for the time spent in the comfortable old rocker by the window, waiting for him to show up.

Even if I haven't hung the feeder by the time the hummers are here next spring, they'll be looking for it. They'll fly right to the spot where I have made a point of hanging it every spring. They've done it before, seeming to remember from one season to the next where they'll find it waiting for them.

The First Hummingbird

I know I'm guilty of rushing the season, but I'm going to keep on doing it. I may not be the only one, what with the balmy weather we've been finding so much more enjoyable than the kind that strains our patience the way one did in early April not long ago. That was when we waited for several inches of snow to melt and freeze again before disappearing after what seemed the interminable length of time it finally spent turning into slush and at last leaving us with history we still recall with a shudder.

Meantime, I have started glancing backward every time I leave the living room to go through the house. It's a good thing I can follow a reasonably clear path, for many times my eyes are glued not to where I'm headed, but to the out of doors. That's because I don't want to run the risk of missing even one lonely little hummingbird that might have arrived to prospect for the food I'm invariably told I've put out too soon in spite of the evidence convincing me I really did it in the nick of time.

As I've admitted before, I do hang the hummingbird feeders in early April, and I look at them many times a day through my living room windowpanes. I've done more than that. For several years, I've made a note on my calendar stating that a hummingbird paused here on the fifteenth of April. I've never seen one before that, nor have I had to wait longer for one to come. It's April 15 always, just as though the bird had a way of knowing.

Although I can barely imagine the size of a brain inside such a tiny head as that of a hummingbird, and one that obviously functions adequately, I was struck by it one day when I was sitting on the porch. A late spell of quite chilly weather had delayed my hanging the feeders, but the near approach of spring was with us again, and right on time the first hummer I saw that year zoomed across the yard in front of me, its wings whirring continuously to keep it airborne. It paused close to the feeder and then veered to one side, and for the slightest moment, it perched on my shoulder as if to show appreciation for what I had provided. For the rest of the summer, I was completely ignored, but the feeder was in continuous attendance.

I still have trouble believing how ill tempered a hummingbird is accused of being, although of such diminutive size. Once a person I knew caught one in his bare hand, and he had visible and painful, and quite regrettable, evidence of it. Yet our appreciation of the bird would soar if we could even estimate the number of insects it eliminates for us, but we seldom give that a thought.

Hummers don't pay much attention to people, but I was flattered beyond all reason the day one lit on my shoulder and, for a brief moment, turned its head far enough toward my neck to put its pointed beak so alarmingly close to my jugular vein that I was thankful its nature didn't allow it to tarry in one position, and in that one in particular, for any length of time.

I can't help wondering, though, if that bird had come to my porch because it remembered the particular feeder hanging there. I'm getting the feeders out now. I'm not about to keep the hummers waiting.

The BIG Hummingbird

People have their "druthers," and a special one of mine is birds. Just ask anyone who knows, feeders are in my yard beyond the windows close to my favorite chair. The birds are abundant all year long, looking after themselves whether or not they stop at the feeders I keep out for them, but they do stop, especially during a migrating season such as we're going through now. An unfamiliar specimen is likely to show up any time, and that was what I saw happening a short time ago.

Knowing a hummingbird has always come on the fifteenth of April, I'd put out my feeders a couple of days ahead of it. Sure enough, I was still idling over my wake-up cup of coffee when a hummer flew against my windowpane. Or I assumed it was a hummer, but for its particular speed and the way it zoomed, I couldn't get a close enough look at it to be certain. But a hummer that size? Yet I was well aware of, and had made numerous references to, the hummers' habitual arrival at this time of the year. Too, a couple of people have called to tell me they've just had hummers. So I crawled out of bed in spite of having had no responses to my periodic information about hummers ever having been received with recognizable enthusiasm.

Then it happened. A few days ago, suddenly a hummingbird noticeably larger than the little ones I'm accustomed to was making its way across my windowpane. I'd never seen one quite like it, although it had all of the characteristics familiar to me. But it was bigger. Lots bigger. And it was almost black, except for the bright red spot on the underside of its neck. I didn't take my eyes off of it—until from my bedroom window I saw a certain member of my family (who shall prudently remain nameless) walk by. I knew he had a key to the front door and could let himself in to see that I'd made it through the night, as he always does. He came in and called to me, asking if any hummingbirds had come, and then he left me to get up and to wonder how many chores had been left undone while, instead of the work he hadn't been doing at all, he had been laboriously fashioning a fake bird with its gossamer wings ready for flight.

With feeling that spring had actually come, it being the middle of April, I finished my second cup of coffee and then left my bed, shoving my winter garments aside in the closet in search of more appropriate attire. I turned off the radio when the announcer predicted snow in the higher elevations and reveled in thankfulness that we were in the lower ones. And one of my granddaughters was calling from Boone to tell me she had just heard of my having hummingbirds. Obviously, she had heard about it instantaneously.

I'll probably get a call from the one in Ecuador any time now with word traveling the way it seems to be doing these days.

Never mind the inches of grass waiting to be mowed, I can just push my winter clothes aside until the "iffiness" of spring is over and the real warmth creeps in. Anyway, I would rather watch the birds at feeders outside my window and the hummers zooming to the front porch ones to make up for fasting during the long flights from Florida and even Mexico.

I can marvel at how those diminutive birds know the direct route to the sugar water I've put out for them when I don't always know how to find some certain place on a short side street in my hometown.

Squirrels

I have no idea how many squirrels I'm nourishing with sunflower seeds that fall from my birdfeeders. I put up a squirrel baffle, but it in no way deterred them. Then one day, I snapped a good picture of a raccoon enjoying a feast so much that he didn't mind the camera at all, nor the fact that I had leaned way out the window in order to get a close-up of him. Another day, a bear was so near the window overlooking the feeders that I could have reached out and patted him on his head. I could have, but I didn't. Then the time came when I had to refill the four cylindrical feeders so often that I had to do something about it. I now have a raccoon baffle on the pole the feeders hang from, and neither raccoons nor squirrels can jump over it. They have to be satisfied with seeds falling on the ground while birds are feasting. The squirrels and I do get close to one another, or at least we're somewhat friendly by now, but I prudently avoid tampering with their independence. There was a time I didn't.

When my sister was a college student, one day she walked underneath a lofty oak tree and on the ground, right at her feet, was a lone baby squirrel. It had fallen out of a nest high in the tree, and young as it was, it stood no chance of climbing back up. Nor was it old enough to provide food for itself. My sister picked it up and took it to her room in the college dormitory. She bought a little bottle with a nipple on it just the right size for a small doll's mouth. Milk was available from the kitchen, and time between classes enabled her to feed her little squirrel. During classes it stayed in her room, sleeping most of the time.

When summer vacation came, she brought the little squirrel home with her and turned it loose in the yard, where trees were plentiful. It frolicked

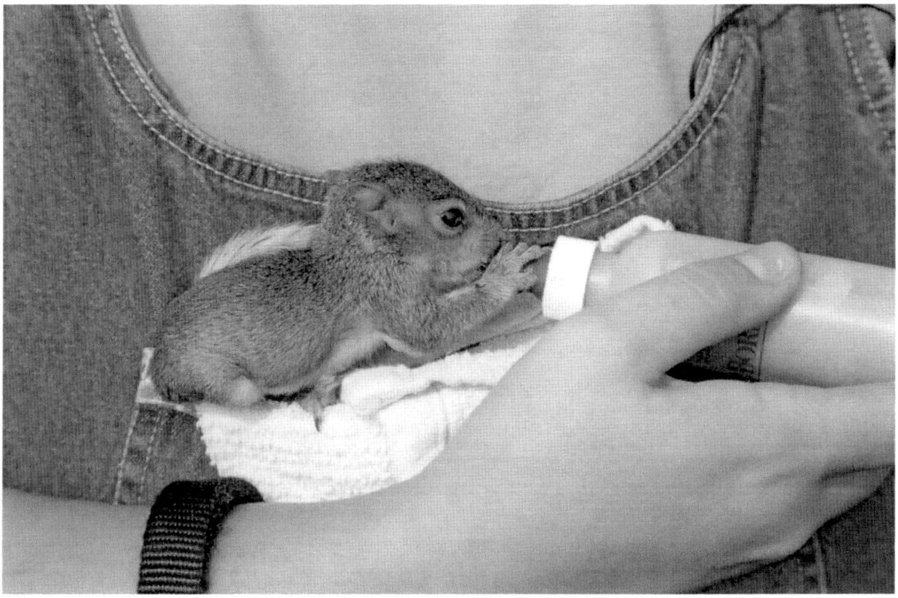

An infant gray squirrel nurses from a doll's bottle. *Photo by Terry Ruscin.*

about among the limbs, but she had only to call its name—which was "So What," but don't ask me why—and it came scampering to her and climbed to her shoulder. I made friends with the little fellow and loved showing off our rapport to friends who dropped by. I was delighted when a cousin—a medical student on holiday—came to see us. My sister was in the yard with So What on her shoulder. Naturally, I had to demonstrate my congeniality with one of Nature's own, so I put out my hand for him to jump onto it.

He jumped all right. He landed with his teeth in the fleshy base of my thumb, and it was as though four oversized hypodermic needles had gone in at once. But they didn't come right out. So What held them there for a few highly impressive and memorable moments, and then he released me and scampered up a tree.

I rushed to the nearest faucet with my cousin at my heels, and I scrubbed the punctures with enough soap to defy infection, and in due time the pain subsided. But So What and I were never friends after that, and he finally abandoned all of us for companionship with the many creatures of his kind in the woods.

It doesn't bother me that squirrels freeload on seeds that get scattered on the ground while birds are feeding. I just don't plan to try to make pets out of them.

CAROLINA WRENS

Granted a bird doesn't "think," according to our interpretation of the word. But our Carolina wrens, for example, wouldn't be such busy little creatures if they didn't have ever so many things to see to between daylight and dark. You don't find them just sitting on a twig as though waiting for something to happen, such as an insect flying within their reach or a newly filled feeder that was empty longer than it should have been—and will empty again sooner than you think.

There's nothing quiet about those little wrens. They're loud. Almost as loud as a raucous crow in spite of the difference in size, but thankfully their notes are more musical, with their variety of pleasing chirps and high-pitched, trilling vocal runs birders call chirrs. It was those chirrs that had me peering through a windowpane one day to see what in the world was causing a disturbance in the hedge growing against the wall of the house.

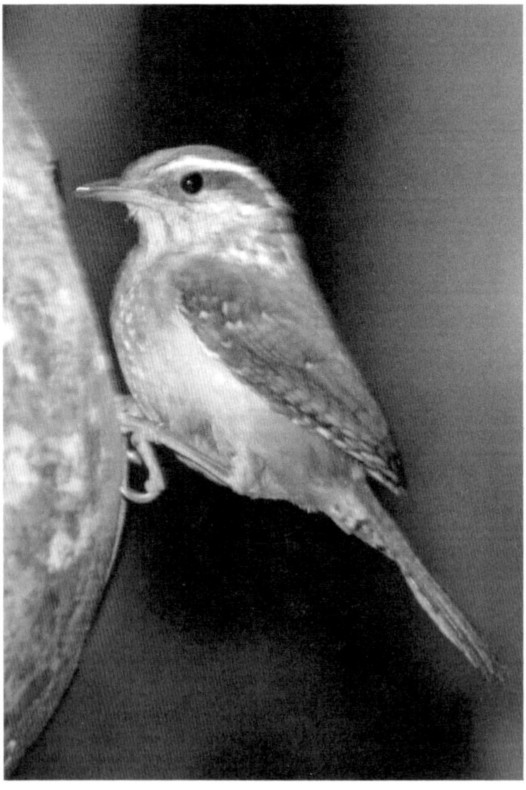

A Carolina wren at a nesting gourd. *Photo by Terry Ruscin.*

At first I couldn't see any sign of life in those bushes, but with my face plastered against the glass, I kept on looking until I finally saw a twig vibrate ever so slightly. Sure enough, a wren was perched on the twig, and all of the sounds were his. He was quivering as though something frightened him, yet he was alone, and there was nothing to keep him from flying away from whatever was upsetting him. He was facing away from my house and looking across the yard, where an iron pole ordinarily stood with four feeders hanging from it. I saw that there were only three. Obviously, the wren knew one was missing, and he was upset.

One of the feeders was lying on the ground. The cord it was supposed to hang by had broken, but since the feeder wasn't full to the brim and the lid had stayed on even when it hit the ground, a minimum of seeds had fallen out. I could easily tell that, with the feeder landing on its side, it would have been impossible for a beak no longer than a wren's to reach as far in as the seeds were. For some reason, the wren ignored the feeders still hanging and easily available, and he kept up what sounded to me like a warning of certain doom.

The only thing I could do was pick up the fallen feeder and hang it back in place, which was what I did, and at that very moment, even with me standing right beside the bush where the wren was, he hushed. I haven't heard a single wren since, and their habits being what they are, I don't expect to hear one until spring. I know he, as well as others of his ilk, are still around, though, not being migratory. In fact, he's bound to be among several of his kind dining fairly amicably with a flock of cardinals but having no tolerance for the blue jays that threaten his domain.

My raccoon baffle is still most effective, and the bear that tried to climb the pole to get to the birdfeeders gave up and has apparently moved on to my neighbors' premises. But the Carolina wrens keep coming for the black-oil sunflower seeds I put out, and I'll be eagerly awaiting their chirps when their instincts let them know it's time to signal the early days of spring.

"Thinking" is hardly the appropriate word for what makes the little wren follow the same pattern from one year to the next. But the regularity with which he goes about it might be a good example of self-discipline.

Ladybugs

It wouldn't have helped my reputation as a housekeeper if someone had come calling on a certain day a week or so ago. Things were pretty much in order, though, such as furniture being in place, a layer of dust not yet settled enough to be noticed by a casual eye and a fair amount of paperwork needing to be attended to being just before, thankfully not just after, getting spread across the dining room table. No visitors arrived, though, so I went to my favorite chair—the one that affords a view through a double window directly out to the birdfeeders hanging where a quick glance can let me know whether something exotic is pausing for nourishment on its way to winter quarters. I could barely see the feeders. The windowpanes, which don't exactly sparkle but afford me a satisfactory view of the yard beyond them, were clouded by myriad little yellow dots with dark dots among the yellow ones.

I've seen plenty of ladybugs over the years, maybe one or two at a time, maybe a thin procession of them climbing up a windowpane. But not until that day had so many of them appeared at once that they blocked out much of the light that should have been coming through the glass. I'd never paid close attention to individual ladybugs, either, but I made a point of doing so while scraping what must have been several colonies of them from the windowsill and tossing them out of doors.

I even took time to pay particular attention to what I'd removed from the windowpane that day, and I was surprised to find no visible heads on the little bugs. Heads were there, of course, and a closer look revealed them, but they were retracted underneath the front end of the dorsal shell, and believe me, they were not easy to see.

It occurred to me that if all that many ladybugs were living on my premises, and I know far less about their habits than it seemed to me I should, I'd better become informed. So I went to my book on insects. I learned that not only are our ladybugs worldwide, but also the good they do has been known since the Middle Ages, when they were dedicated to the Virgin Mary. Even that long ago it was known that both larvae and adults fed on aphids that would otherwise rob useful plants of beneficial juices or spread diseases among them.

You can distinguish ladybugs from similar beetles that frequent gardens because, for one thing, their legs are shorter. Too, they lay their eggs on plants affected by aphids and scale, the latter living in colonies on plants with succulent juices such as fruit trees and ornamental plants. Ladybugs are the highly effective enemies of the aphids and scale.

Since I'm not a gardener, I seldom look at the underside of leaves. If I did, I would likely see little bunches of ladybug eggs attached to many of them. I haven't seen the little wormlike hatchlings either, visible though they are in their search for plant lice, which they eagerly devour and thereby offer a real service to a gardener.

For anyone who may wonder why a person would spend time learning the ways of a mere little ladybug, the answer is simple. Even the tiniest, and perhaps the most insignificant creature, in one way or another plays a part in the lives of us human beings. That's what the ladybug does as it fits into the plan Nature has for it.

Katydid, Katydidn't

During summer evenings, my father always sat on his split-log bench on the front porch and relaxed after the day inside his office in Hendersonville. He liked to listen to the sounds of Nature and to see the changes that came about as summer wore on. But when the fifteenth of July came, we didn't need a calendar to remind us, for he never failed to tell us, with noticeable relief in his voice, "the backbone of summer is broken."

Daddy liked to think about it right after he heard a katydid, the first sound of that particular relative of the grasshopper, for he knew there would soon be great numbers of katydids frequenting the trees around us and alerting us to their whereabouts by loud, high-pitched calls that seemed to say "katydid, katydidn't." They made the calls by stridulating, which my father left to Webster's dictionary to describe as a sound made by a structure at the base of a wing cover and resulting from friction when one part of it is rubbed against the other. According to Webster's, the sound can be heard for half a mile, even though the entire insect is only a couple or so inches long. Females chirp, while the males answer with their stridulating.

At first, the katydids are here only after dark, but as time goes on, a few, and eventually myriad of them, stridulate in late daytime as well. And it's

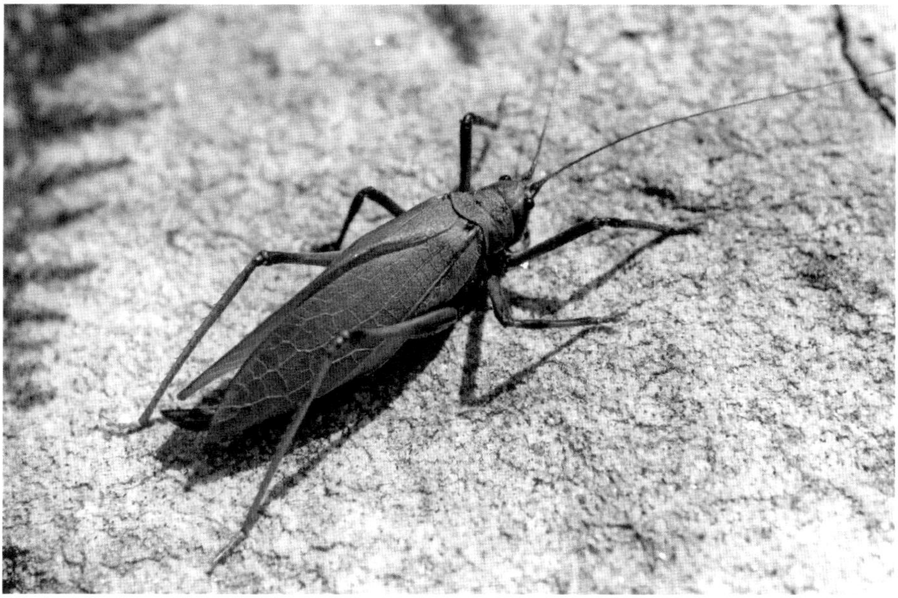

Katydid. *Photo by Terry Ruscin.*

when we hear them before dark that we know summer will soon take its place in history. A particular child visiting us from the city never seemed to be disturbed by, if even aware of, the automobiles passing her house at all hours, but she was unable to fall asleep during her visit when katydids stridulated outside my windows.

When summer residents from south of us returned home as their children's schools opened, my dad could drive the four miles from home to his office behind few other automobiles, even on the highway. I don't remember his ever trying to pass anyone else, for he left early enough to avoid getting in a hurry. Little River Road, still unpaved then, wasn't wide enough for passing anyway. Trenholm Road was even narrower. He just made sure he had plenty of time for his speed of ten miles an hour over the bumpy dirt road and little more than twice that after he reached the hard-surfaced highway.

For a while in summer, my dad still had plenty of time to relax on the front porch after his long days in the office, although the idea of daylight saving time was still a long way off. He could enjoy his Sunday afternoons when his cousin Middleton came to have dinner with us, which he did for as long as I can remember. And during their conversations on the sunny porch afterward, "Middie," as we called him, sitting on a split-log bench with his head resting against a stone pillar, invariably fell asleep. As busy as his small farm kept him, that time with us seemed right for the additional rest he needed.

A few nights ago, I heard katydids exactly on time: July 15. Cool weather has held back some of them, but Nature has its pattern. If you notice sourwood leaves showing red on the edges, Indian pipes fading along roadside banks and goldenrod not far from blossoming, you'll know why, for, as my father used to say at this time of the year, "the backbone of summer is broken."

And I still find myself noticing the signs of it as they come about.

Bullfrogs

We've had dry spells before. One August, the leaves on Glassy Mountain's trees began to turn brown, and those of us depending on wells for our water supply were limited to two-inch-deep baths. Not enough rain fell to leave puddles in the yard, and worse yet, there seemed to be far fewer bullfrogs croaking around the pond. The charm of evenings in the country was threatened.

Because I had always enjoyed sitting on the porch on summer evenings and listening to the bullfrogs' "jug-a-rumming," I became concerned over

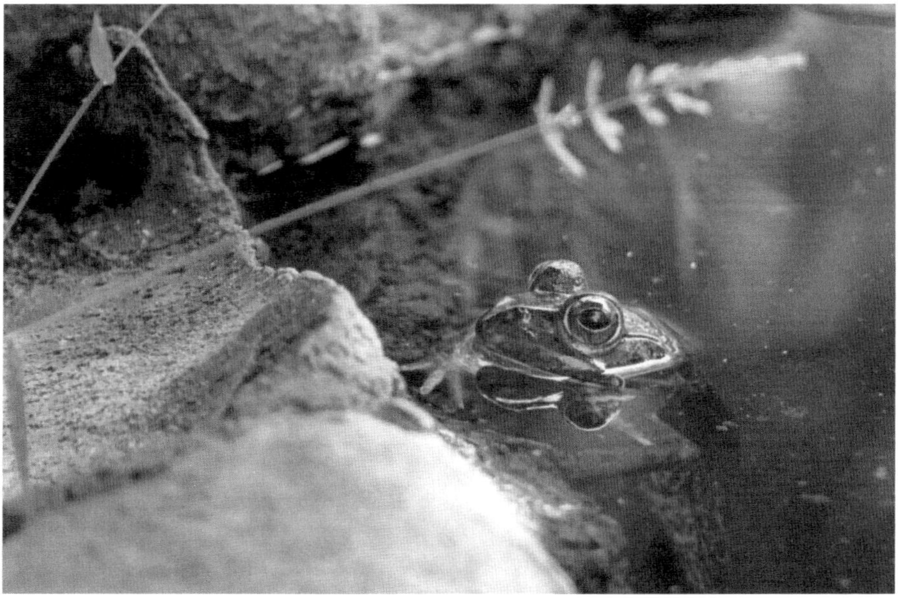

A bullfrog warily observes the photographer. *Photo by Terry Ruscin.*

the apparent shortage of them. I mentioned it to people, some of whom could understand why it mattered to me, while others, who had never heard a bullfrog croak and therefore couldn't know what they were missing, changed the subject as quickly as possible. But I could count on my sister. She would see it the way I did.

Up in Virginia where she lives, afternoon showers remained plentiful. Her grass was green, and puddles lingered where no grass grew. It so happened that one of our brothers was going to drive down to visit those of his family in Flat Rock, and he would drop in on our sister on his way. When he arrived at my house, he brought in what was necessary and then he went back to his car "to get," he said, "a little present our sister sent you." I couldn't miss the sly grin he said it through.

You may think you know what perpetual motion is, but I assure you, you haven't really seen it until you're handed a quart jar with water up to the brim and two-thirds of the water teeming with tadpoles and pollywogs not yet old enough even to hint at becoming toads and bullfrogs but active enough to make you cross-eyed if you try to follow the motions of a single one, much less a quart of them. My thoughtful sister had jabbed holes in the lid of the jar so the creatures wouldn't suffocate but too small to let an appreciable amount of water splash out of the jar and into our brother's car. There wasn't a casualty in the lot.

What happened to them after they were emptied into my pond, I had no way of knowing until the evening serenades increased in volume as they issued from far more voices than I had been hearing before.

My sister doesn't have a pond at her home in Virginia. She does have puddles after heavy rains, and it was out of one of them that she had ladled up the tadpoles and pollywogs. Fortunately, her premises have more sand than clay, for the little critters would have been hard to see in muddy water. And she had warned our brother to be sure the jar didn't turn over in transit, which he would have done anyway rather than risk having to pick up all of its squirming contents before they expired.

I listen to bullfrogs on summer evenings now and think of my sister's thoughtfulness toward all kinds of creatures. I think of a time she was "cat sitting" overnight for a daughter who had a host of cats that paraded in and out of the house twenty hours a day. Rather than getting up to accommodate each cat, my sister left the door open for their convenience. A raccoon walked in. My sister woke up to find it sitting on the foot of her bed. "Leave it alone," she said. "It'll go away."

And it did, but she didn't know just when, nor did she care. She left it sitting there and went right on back to sleep.

THE BLACK GUM TREE

It won't be long now until splashes of red and gold appear on roadsides, hinting that autumn is only a breath away. My household used to see the earliest signs of it, for a black gum tree stood beside our driveway on the edge of the front yard.

It wasn't a pretty tree, except in autumn when the leaves turned from a commonplace shade of green to scarlet. In no way does it resemble a dogwood, although it belongs to the dogwood family, a family with specimens sometimes reaching a height of one hundred feet, though the black gum seldom grows that high in our area. The one beside our driveway never came anywhere near it and was, in fact, too small to attract much attention at all.

When we thought winter was over, we watched for leaf buds to appear on the black gum tree. And in April, inconspicuous greenish flower clusters became noticeable, though leaves coming out on the trees were not yet fully grown. Dark blue berries on long stems matured in autumn, and birds, especially bluebirds, feasted on them.

I passed by our black gum tree every time I went up or down our driveway, seeing it clearly but giving no thought to it at all until the judge came to visit us.

The judge, a relative of ours living in Virginia, had retired, and at last he could spend an appreciable amount of time with us. I was a teenager tagging along on the many drives taken to show him the four corners of our county and, at times, sitting with him in the car while my dad was seeing a patient in a house tucked away on a mountainside.

One day, the judge—who, by the way, had always lived in the city—came back from his daily walk along our driveway. He called me into the yard and pointed to a tree that had caught his attention. He said he would reward me with a box of candy if I could tell him what kind of tree it was. I knew it was the black gum, for my dad never failed to remind me jokingly every time we passed it that I must be sure not to forget it. So I identified the tree for the judge but spared him details of how I knew. When my dad drove into the yard that evening, the judge ordered me to wait on the porch. He didn't even wait until my dad was out of the car before he pointed to the tree and asked what kind it was. My dad told him right off, "Why, that's a black gum tree."

It has been too long now to remember, but I probably ate the whole box of candy myself. I'd never had such an opportunity before.

I haven't the faintest recollection of how, why or when that tree was removed, but it has been gone for many years now. I don't know whether it had begun to shrink from old age the way black gums are supposed to do. What I do know, and harbor the most pleasant memories of, is how my family gathered by the fireplace on chilly autumn evenings. We'll be having evenings like that before long now. I know there are black gum trees out in my woods waiting to show off splashes of color. I would like to walk among them, but I know, too, there are bears out in those woods. And coyotes. Maybe I'll just stay in the yard—about where that special black gum tree of ours used to stand.

Carolina Characters

Home Schooling With Peg

I don't know anything about the home schooling that goes on nowadays. I do know how our cousin Peg [Margaret Campbell] launched my sister Jennie and me into education, although she had had no training at all, and I have no recollection of her ever mentioning having gone to college. I know, though, that when she came from Charleston to spend summers at Argyle, her grandfather's Flat Rock summer home, she taught reading, writing and arithmetic to neighborhood children, one of whom told me in much later years, "Hit 'us the onliest education we got." There was no school near enough for them to attend it, nor could they have taken time for it when they were needed to help keep the summer houses and gardens in good shape.

Peg was living with our family when Jennie turned six. She spent each weekday morning teaching Jennie, and I—two years younger—felt so painfully neglected while the lessons were going on that I made enough of a nuisance of myself that, finally, Peg allowed me to sit on her lap when Jennie was reading. For my benefit, Peg pointed to the words as Jennie read them, and since Peg taught her to read the words phonetically, I learned them that way too. Because I liked the name Elizabeth, although with the lisp I had at the time I pronounced it "Elithabeth," and because my doll had a small head, my father suggested I add Microcephalous, meaning small head. So, with the lisp, my doll became "Elithabeth Microthephaluth," and of course my father prompted me to tell the name to everyone who came our way.

We didn't have compulsory education then. Many children out in the county were long past the age of six when they started to school, for they

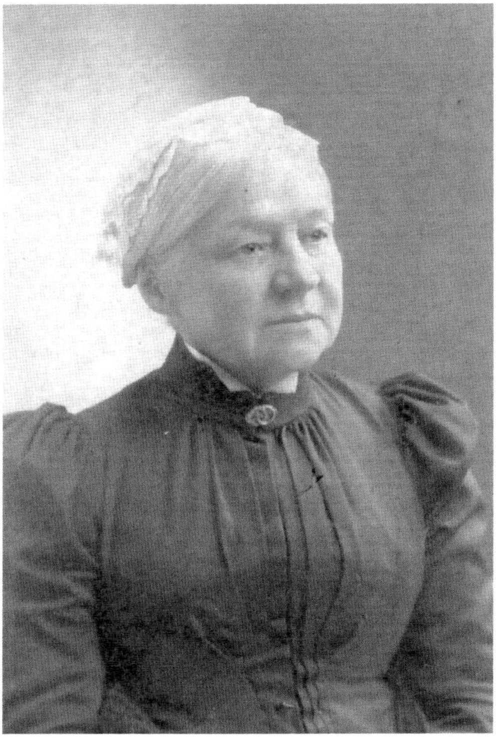

Cousin Peg (Margaret Campbell). *Photo courtesy of Joseph Bailey Jr.*

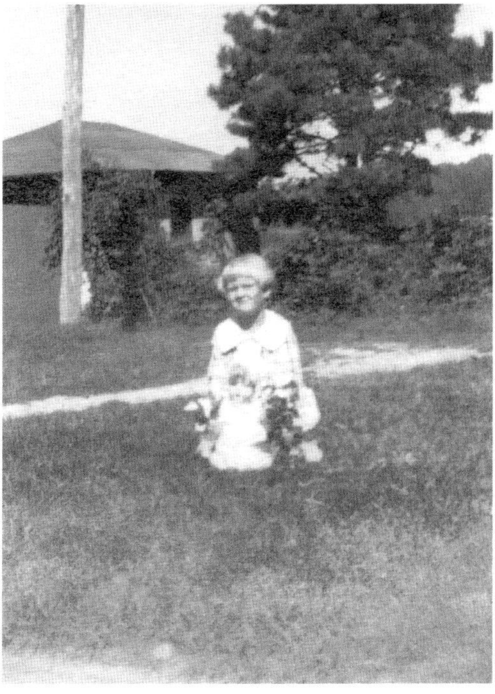

Louise with her doll, Elizabeth. *Photo courtesy of Joseph Bailey Jr.*

were needed to help work on the farms. Education had to wait until there was time to pursue it. I attended a homecoming dinner at a mountain church when I was six, and the preacher asked if one of the young folks would like to read the psalm. The person who had taken me there didn't ask me if I would like to; she simply announced that I would do it, and I knew I'd better in spite of shyness that almost made me speechless.

Thanks to Peg, I had no trouble pronouncing the words, though. She had drilled phonics into me before the "look-see" method of reading required tackling the entire word at a glance instead of sounding out each syllable in its turn, as Peg had taught me to do. Emphasis didn't always land on the syllable it was supposed to, but juggling it into its rightful place—and its right form—would come in due time.

I've always hoped it did for a student I taught in a biology class when he was in his second year of high school. On a particular test, he was asked to follow the course of the arterial system. He wrote:

> *The tempeal is in the head and keeps the head from bleeding all but the face. The facial is in the jaw and keeps the face from bleeding. One is on the Adam's appeal and stops bleeding from neck up and the Breakel stops the arm from bleed about half way between the elbo and sholder.*

I knew the lad and his lifestyle on a farm, where experience had taught him how to handle situations involving the arteries. Peg would have had a harder time drilling correct spelling and grammar into him than he would have had rising to an emergency.

Growing Up with Carolyn

You can imagine how delighted I was when my friend Carolyn [Smith Lockaby] told her family she wanted to celebrate her ninety-fifth birthday with a visit to me. That meant her daughter and son-in-law would drive from Due West, South Carolina, to Seneca to pick her up, and from Seneca to Flat Rock, and then back to Due West after our visit. But they did it cheerfully, and we met over at Flat Rock's deli. A two-hour lunch barely gave us time to recall the highlights of the eighty-one years we've been friends.

We had met at Fassifern School, day students among a host of boarders whose campus activities rarely included us, who were free to leave as soon as our last class was over. Carolyn spent more Friday nights and Saturdays at

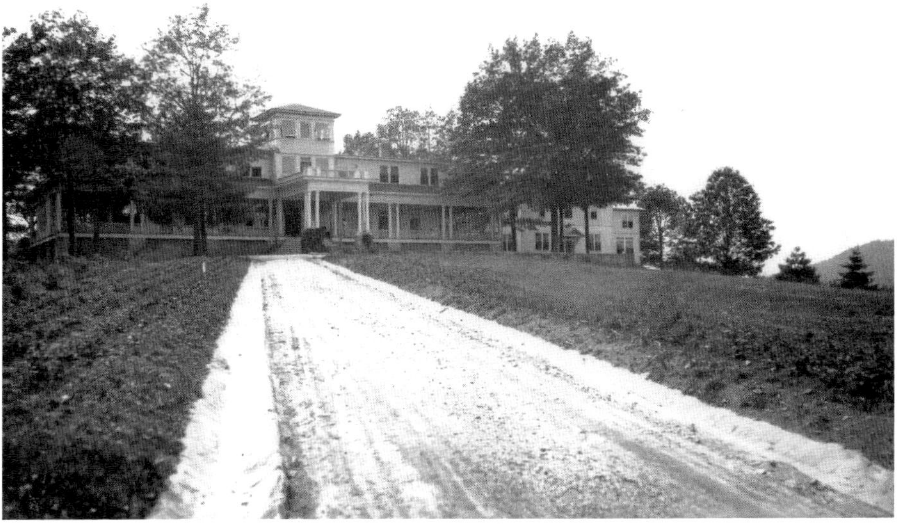

Fassifern School for Girls, Hendersonville. *Photo courtesy of the Henderson County Genealogical and Historical Society, Inc.*

my house than at her own, although I spent some with her when her family lived at Killarney, the spacious stone house on Killarney Street designed by my grandfather and now on the National Register of Historic Places. Sometimes we walked from there through town and on out to my house on Little River Road. Other times, if Lady, my family's horse—beyond her prime as a saddle horse—wasn't being used for plowing, or our caretaker didn't need her to pull his wagon into town, I rode her to Carolyn's house. Carolyn climbed on behind the saddle for the five-mile ride to my house.

Usually we went down Main Street and reined in at Hunter's Pharmacy on the corner of Main and Fifth Avenue West. Curb service was popular then, and it didn't matter if no parking space was available. A horse doesn't need a lot of room, so we squeezed in between cars and waited aboard while the soda jerk brought us a couple of cherry smashes. Each of us paid our nickel, and we rode away enjoying our drinks as we traveled—and hoped Lady's iron shoes wouldn't slip on the concrete and splash out any of our treat.

During our recent visit, Carolyn reminded me of a particular hike we made up Pinnacle Mountain with my sister Jennie and another girl. Jennie had driven us in our family's car as far up the mountain as the Old CCC Road is now, but at that time it was only a wagon road. Although there would not likely have been anyone passing that way for the next several days, Jennie took out the ignition key and put it in a pocket of the jacket she was wearing. When we reached Ellen Stepp's house, we stopped to visit briefly and then we continued our climb to Pinnacle Rocks at the top of the mountain. After spending time enjoying the magnificent view from the Rocks, we returned to our car, and Jennie reached into her pocket for the key.

There was no key.

Somewhere on the wooded path along the broad, sloping side of Pinnacle, the key had fallen out of her pocket. Jennie did what she had to do. She walked to the nearest telephone to call our dad and ask him to bring us his key. The distance from our car to that telephone measured five miles—and she had already scaled the mountainside.

Carolyn reminded me that she had twisted her ankle on the way down the mountain. "I just took off my leather belt and made a strap out of it. It worked fine," she said, remembering we didn't let many things interfere with our fun back then.

During my visit with Carolyn, I particularly enjoyed watching the expressions on the faces of her daughter and son-in-law. It was as though they couldn't believe how times have changed.

FLOSSIE LEE CANNON

When I needed help looking after my three young sons while my husband Joe was necessarily spending more time with his patients than at home, Flossie had come from her mother's house in South Carolina to visit her cousin in Hendersonville. She needed a job, so her cousin telephoned me, and from the next day until the end of eight years afterward, she was in my previously empty upstairs, on duty five days and nights every week and going back to South Carolina for weekends.

She was young, personable and capable, and we remained friends, although a number of miles have separated us and I'm a stay-at-home. When she was here, she had no automobile and had never learned to drive, but she had a friend who occasionally came up from South Carolina after his work was over in the evenings, and except for his occasional appearance in the kitchen, they visited in his automobile on the far side of the yard. That was her social life.

Although I have no contact with her nowadays, memories are everlasting, and so is appreciation.

Flossie's particular way of speaking reflected more than the characteristic way of many upper South Carolinians. It was spontaneous and generously sprinkled with originality, as was evident one evening when she returned from a trip with her cousin to attend a protracted meeting held in a tent beside the highway into town. According to Flossie, the self-prepared preacher had announced loudly and with an index finger pointing directly to her, "That's a friendly face over there. We want to make that person one of us." Flossie, relieved to be back home when the meeting was over, assured us, "I got that friendly face out o' there, 'cause right then everybody else went to doin' the holy squat."

I would have to see a "holy squat" to get an apt description, never mind an interpretation. I know, though, that if I had seen it, I wouldn't have stayed to participate.

While Flossie expressed certain things in a way that was by no means commonplace, it was well worth hearing her do it, even if you occasionally had to ferret out the gist of her information, as I was doing one day when her message finally became clear. As she passed me on her way to her next chore, she said hurriedly, "I put them goobles back on the hickey." She sped on, and I purposely went into the dining room she'd come through. There I found the silver she had polished gleaming on the sideboard—the hickey, that is, not the doohickey, which would have afforded me a trifle more familiarity.

But that was only part of it. Flossie was never at a loss for words, for they came to her, in whatever fashion, as she needed them.

I don't know if Flossie is still in South Carolina. We have never exchanged letters, and I know a tremor was developing in her hands that would make writing very difficult for her. She never had a telephone in her name, but I treasure the memories.

Miss Lily Logan

I couldn't imagine who would be calling me from New York City a few days ago. When I dialed the number that had been left on my answering machine, a pleasant voice began assuring me I didn't know her, but she was calling to ask if I might possibly have heard of her great-great-great-aunt, who lived in Flat Rock many years ago. I admit antiquity, but a great-great-great-aunt sounded too long ago even for me. Only it wasn't.

I hadn't just heard of the person. I had known her. She was Miss Lily Logan, and her house was just a few doors beyond ours when we lived a scant mile south of town. It's still there, looking very much as it did back then. I pass it almost daily, and I find myself wishing I knew more about Miss Lily, a favorite neighbor of my sister and me when we were children. She moved away when I was nine years old, and we didn't see nor hear of her again—until a few days ago.

I'd known Miss Lily as a nice lady who seemed to have an endless supply of cookies and what I realize now was infinite patience with children. I had no way of knowing—and would not have been impressed at my age by what a busy and rewarding life she had had as an artist in her own country and abroad. I had never seen but one of her paintings. It was a portrait of Fanny Stepp, who lived on Pinnacle Mountain. I never knew Fanny, but the portrait hung in the home of her son and two daughters, and I saw it the many times I visited them.

That Miss Lily would choose Fanny Stepp for a model attests to her insight into the character portrayed in the face of a true mountain woman. That Miss Lily would attempt to preserve that character on canvas was recognition of her effort to preserve our memory of the special mountain culture. But accomplishing it on canvas could not have been easy for Miss Lily. Fanny lived well beyond the beaten path. A wagon road leading to her house was passable enough in dry spells, but anyone afraid to take an automobile over it was obliged to walk the uphill mile. Yet it was not strange that Miss Lily could find Fanny's house on the mountainside, for climbing Pinnacle was a favorite outing for Flat Rock summer residents. Miss Lily was a friend of all of them, but for her the outing was purposeful as well. She carried her artist's equipment with her.

The heavy gold frame holding Fanny's portrait would have been beyond a price the sisters and their brother could pay, but Miss Lily hung it in their house just the same. It hung as one of the two pictures on their wall. The other was a photograph of one of Fanny's granddaughters, a beautiful girl who died while still young.

Miss Lily's great-great-great-niece wrote a note to me saying she is considering hopping on a plane and coming down from New York to see the places I could show her. I hope she does, and I shall take her first to see the portrait painted by her relative. But before she comes, I have some reading to do. She has sent me a forty-seven-page record of her Logan relatives, beginning with the ones who came to Charleston in the 1700s. The names could well be a roster of those Charlestonians who were Flat Rock's summer residents for many years.

Dr. J.S. Brown

Dr. Brown
Office hours
8 a.m.–12 Noon
1 p.m. – 6 p.m.
Or As Suits

If all of the babies delivered by Dr. James Steven Brown stood side by side along Main Street, the line would reach from one end of town to the other and then some. According to him, "There were somewhere between six and seven thousand babies when I quit counting." It was no wonder that, in 1948, the American Medical Association awarded a gold medal to Dr. Brown, "who has won universal recognition for exceptional service as a general practitioner."

Three years earlier, Dr. Brown had undergone surgery followed by a period of hospitalization. As he stated in his fourteen-page "Bits of Autobiography":

> *After three long months they let me wobble out under regulatory restrictions, i.e., never more to drive a car (and I haven't driven much over 50,000 miles since); see no night patients (and I have seen only those who needed a doctor's help); do no more obstetrics (but my count has increased from 5786 to 6080). Thanks to three excellent surgeons, with kind help from a skilled dietitian and a lovely nurse…and my ever-present Guardian Angels, I have no ambition to retire from work while there are any good deeds for me to do.*

Many of Dr. Brown's patients lived beyond where a car could possibly go, but he never refused a call, even when he was obliged to go part of the way on foot, and once up a steep, muddy hill on his hands and knees. Many of his patients could not afford payment, but he willingly went when help was needed and always with the conviction that people would pay him when—or if—they could.

Dr. Brown had brought a new era to the medical community in Henderson County when he came with obstetrical instruments and chloroform and a use of them that established him as the leading obstetrician in Western North Carolina. Some other doctors have delivered triplets, but Dr. Brown perhaps holds the record for having brought three sets of them into the world. Before Patton Memorial—Henderson County's first hospital—was built in 1913, he took seriously ill children into his large stone house, which stood on the Greenville Highway south of town.

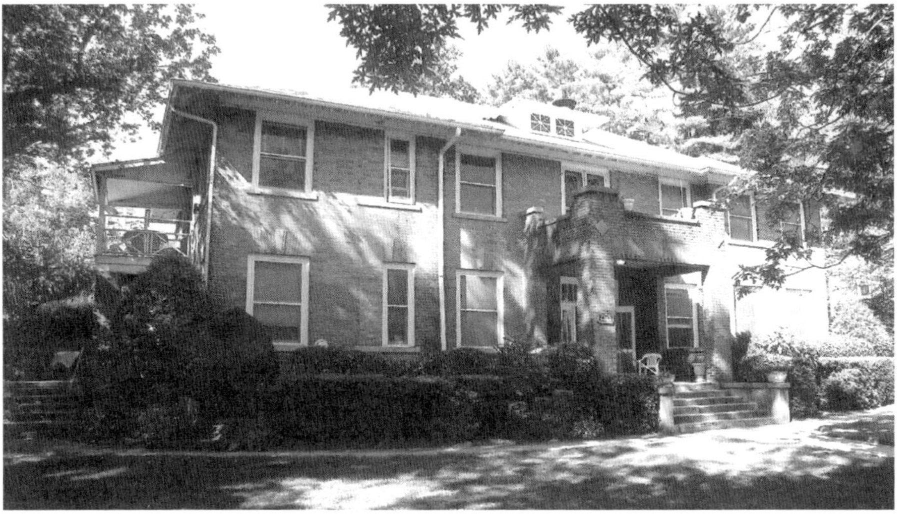

Patton Memorial Hospital (predecessor of Pardee Hospital), Hendersonville. *Photo by Terry Ruscin.*

Dr. Brown must have welcomed the automobile as a great timesaver and a far more comfortable conveyance than a buggy or horseback, and road conditions never deterred him. Once in his early eighties, making a call on a country road, his car became hopelessly stuck, yet he refused help. He dragged a pile of brush into the deep rut and jammed it as far under the wheels as he could. Then, according to a bystander, "He took off in low gear, knocking down a couple of fence posts and leaving part of a fender in the process." But he was determined to get to his patient.

He did have a certain amount of trouble with fenders. When he sheared one from a car he was passing on one of the streets in town, through his open window he called to the driver, "You fix yours; I'll fix mine." The officer to whom the driver complained said, "That's our good Dr. Brown going to save a life or bring one into the world." And he waved the driver on.

Dr. Brown practiced medicine for sixty-five years, most of that time right here in Henderson County.

FLAT ROCK FARRIER

You have to be an old-timer to have played on the nine-hole golf course in Flat Rock in the early 1900s or to have known the Markley family who had a blacksmith shop on Blue Ridge Road. Yet the Markleys were probably the busiest people in the whole community.

Captain Ellison Adger Smyth, formerly of Charleston, had put the golf course on his hill at Connemara for his family and friends to enjoy. It was a bit unusual, though, for in order to make it fit into the available space, it began and ended with the same hole, the ninth hole being the same as the first one.

Special memories still linger among Flat Rock residents who took their horses to be shod at the Markleys' blacksmith shop on the sharp bend on Blue Ridge Road. When the summer season opened and families from Charleston, Savannah and New Orleans flocked to their Flat Rock summer houses, work for the Markleys became so heavy that Jim, who had followed his father as the farrier, was obliged to close for two hours in the middle of the day to rest from handling impatient horses. Jim's father had been the first mail carrier in Flat Rock, as well as a farrier, and for a time Jim had served after him, walking effortlessly with the mail in a sack over his shoulder, for there was not a great deal of it.

Lads took the horses to Markleys' shop and waited while the shoeing was going on. What they liked even better than watching Jim's skilled hands at work were the stories he told and the special way he had of telling them. He

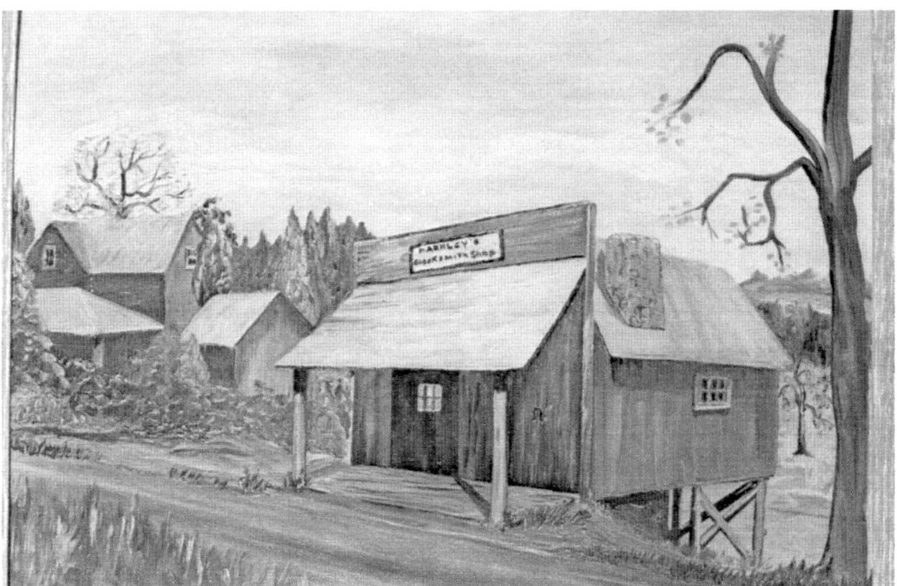

The Markley Blacksmith Shop at Flat Rock from an original oil painting by Clarence A. Peace. The structure was torn down in the late 1960s. *Postcard courtesy of C.E. and Debby Staton.*

did it in what he called "rabbit talk," strange syllables he claimed only he and the rabbits could understand. And when a horse, especially a spirited one, grew tired of standing on three hooves while the fourth one was being shod, Jim took care of the problem with a twitch, a short stick with a rope loop on it that he could slip over the horse's nose. Then he had a couple of the oldest boys standing by take hold of the ends of the twitch and turn it just enough to let the horse know he'd better stand still.

Fire in Jim's forge was always red-hot—ready to heat a shoe until the steel could be molded to match the shape of the particular hoof it was meant for. Sparks flew during the heating, and once a lad standing too close had a piece of metal go down the front of his shirt. He bent over and waited to stand up again until the sliver had burned through the coarse material of his shirt.

A farmer's son, now a man recalling his youth, says that when he was only ten or twelve years old, he was sent to take two teams of workhorses to Jim Markley to be shod. He rode one of the horses, a powerful Percheron, and led the others. Then, while Jim was taking time out for lunch and a rest afterward, he, too, went for a snack. He went to Peace's Grocery, now the Wrinkled Egg, and bought his own lunch of soda crackers and a "dope," as Coca-Colas were called then.

He knew he would have no trouble taking the four horses back home. He was just glad his grandmother's Copper Lady wasn't among them, for when Copper Lady was shod, two strong boys had to hold onto the reins to keep her still. Once she was able to turn toward Connemara, though, there was no way to hold her back. She knew she was going *home*.

GEORGE A. TRENHOLM

Someday I'm going to gather up all of the loose papers lying on tables, shelves and desks in my house. Then I'm going to borrow a wheelbarrow and make as many trips as necessary to cart them down to where I can burn them without alarming my neighbors. All that's left will be a little pile of ashes that time and a few high winds will relegate to oblivion.

I've set out to do it on several occasions but haven't managed to get beyond the good intentions that have mounted along with the stack of papers, be they typed, handwritten or professionally printed. I just can't do away with memorabilia I may want to refer to in years to come. So I've kept them, firmly believing I, or someone else, will eventually find their information worthwhile or, if merely trivial, perhaps amusing in one way or another.

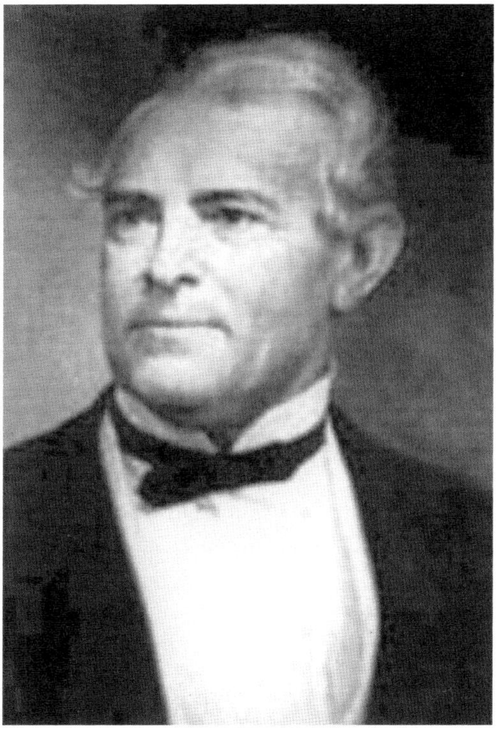

George A. Trenholm. *Photo courtesy of C.E. and Debby Staton.*

So there was no way I could delete from my collection of papers an account written by a daughter of George A. Trenholm, the second secretary of the Confederate treasury. Every time we drive through Flat Rock, we see a memorial to George Trenholm up on the bank where Highland Lake Road comes into Highway 225. At one time, the sign was partially hidden by undergrowth, and someone said, "That doesn't matter, for no one knows who Trenholm was anyway." That person had only recently come to Flat Rock and had a lot to learn about the history of the area, including the fact that George Trenholm had, for a short time, owned property in the little mountain community. And when war was tearing our country apart, his ships ran a successful blockade of Southern ports.

The account smothered in my stack of papers tells of Trenholm's imprisonment twice at Fort Pulaski, then held by Union forces, and of his "endeavor to bear my share of passing trial with fortitude." He viewed his own suffering with the consolation that "it was necessary that some persons in South Carolina would be held to answer if not for her past conduct at least for her future of good conduct." He added that he would be willing to fulfill that duty with cheerfulness.

And right in the middle of his predictions and promises, he took time to write of a most trying situation of everyday life in the coastal area of South Carolina:

> *You see a little blood on the edge of this paper. You can form no idea of the torment we suffer from the mosquitoes. It is almost impossible to write.*

> *Numbers attack your hands, face and neck incessantly, pierce even through your clothes and sting you most venomously in the back. We almost live out of doors with fans in our hands. We can fan and read, but not write. Very little writing has been done for a week past. What we have suffered hitherto from these little miscreants has been nothing compared to what we endure now.*

At George Trenholm's death, one of the tributes paid him stated:

> *It is for such a citizen that the flags of the nation have been drooped. It is for such a son that commerce for a time folds her white wings and is still. Under the majestic branches of a giant oak in our city of the dead is his fit resting place. He sleeps in the soil of his birth, in death as in life adhering to South Carolina.*

When you drive along Highway 225 through Flat Rock, go slowly past the marker honoring this man who was well known among the people who summered in our mountain community.

DINNER AT CEDAR SPRINGS

Walking down the hill after church services a couple of Sundays ago, I raised my umbrella against more of a mist than a rain. The person walking with me knew I'd planned to go right on to a special dinner ten or so miles away, but she supposed that because of the rain I would change my plans.

Not even a frog strangler would have made me do that. I was going to Cedar Springs Church, where a dinner was being held in honor of the Reverend Bill Tinsley, who has spent some fifty years in the ministry. The service had just ended, and men were ignoring the mist as they gathered to welcome one another. Women were hurrying into the fellowship hall to set out a double row of home-cooked meats and vegetables and a gallon or more of "creasy" greens, commonly known as watercress. A table was laden with desserts. I took time to count among my blessings the friends who had telephoned me saying, "Come if you can," and I had made sure I could.

While I was there, my thoughts drifted back to the 1930s, when I had dinner at Cedar Springs for the first time. A few old-timers now, who were then children, can vouch for the fact that I haven't missed many dinners at Cedar Springs between then and now. My dad had bought some mountain land nearby, and several men put up a small log room he could use for a shelter when he went squirrel hunting in the fall. Over the years, I took friends, especially girls from the flatlands, to the cabin to rough it close to the haunts of rattlesnakes. After leading them from the cabin to the top of Pinnacle Mountain and back, they slept well on the bare cabin floor.

I thought about the first time I took my friend Amelia, city born and bred, to spend a couple of days in the cabin.

Amelia had borrowed her brother's yellow convertible with red leather seat covers to drive up from Savannah. At that time, there was only one car in the settlement where my dad's cabin was. Mule teams and wagons provided transportation for folks who couldn't walk the whole way to town. Then a car was bought for use when several people, not just one or two, needed to go to town. Some still walked, taking shortcuts that straightened the miles but were paths rather than roads.

During Amelia's and my stay at the cabin, a revival was going on at Cedar Springs Church, and we attended one evening. She had a beautiful contralto voice and was a soloist in the choir of her Episcopal church in Savannah. But she had never sung in, nor heard, the joyful way of singing that goes on in our mountain churches. She loved to sing, though. I learned a long time ago that for the sake of people around me, I should only mouth, not

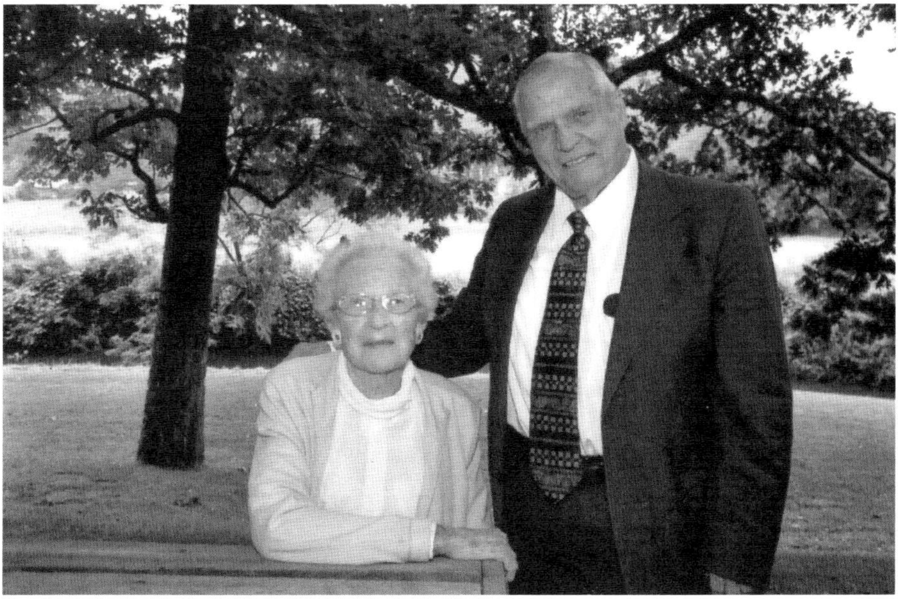

Louise Howe Bailey and the Reverend Bill Tinsley at the 2009 Cedar Springs Baptist Church homecoming picnic—Louise's last. *Photo by Terry Ruscin.*

sound, the words when hymns are sung. If Amelia and I had gone to every meeting of the revival at Cedar Springs, she may have been able to join in the singing, for she did practice both rhythm and tempo in the solitude of the cabin, but the only hymn she actually knew by heart was "Nearer My God to Thee," which wasn't the best one for the purpose.

During that dinner a couple of Sundays ago, little children ran in and out among the grownups. I took another helping of creasy greens to enjoy while I watched them and recalled trips to Cedar Springs way back when Reverend Bill Tinsley had just begun to preach.

Ceph's Illness

My husband, Joe, had just begun his practice as a family physician in Hendersonville when the fair came to town. At that time, his office was at the top of a long flight of steps and down a hall in a building across Second Avenue from the courthouse. I was there to help however I could, which wasn't much because I knew nothing about office procedures, and the closest I had come to nursing was applying a Band-Aid. I couldn't type well, and for a while Joe had plenty of time to take his own telephone calls, a couple of which convinced me that messages were more effective on a one-to-one basis than passed on through an intermediary. Ceph's call was an example.

Ceph telephoned during office hours and explained his condition to the doctor. "I'll give you a suppository to use now," the doctor said. Then, considering further instructions unnecessary, he told Ceph, "If you aren't any better, I'll stop by to see you on my way home this evening." Ceph was feeling a little bit better, although he admitted, "What you sent me is the only thing I've been able to keep on my stummick all day. But Doc, them's the awfullest tastin' things, and I thought I'd never get it swallered."

Remembering that people call with problems very real to them, whoever answers the doctor's phone must listen carefully in order to pass the exact message on to the doctor correctly. That is not always easily done. It wasn't on a certain day when I was supposed to be taking telephone messages and a man on the other end of the line set right in on his problem. "Look," he said, "I've got this risin' on my chest. I put pine tar on it till it came to a head, then I took one o' these here aquarium pumps and pumped out the little blob inside of it. Say, you know how some navels turn in and some turn out? Well, this looks like a turned-out navel. I'm comin' by for the doctor to see it, and I'll bring a jarful o' the stuff when I come."

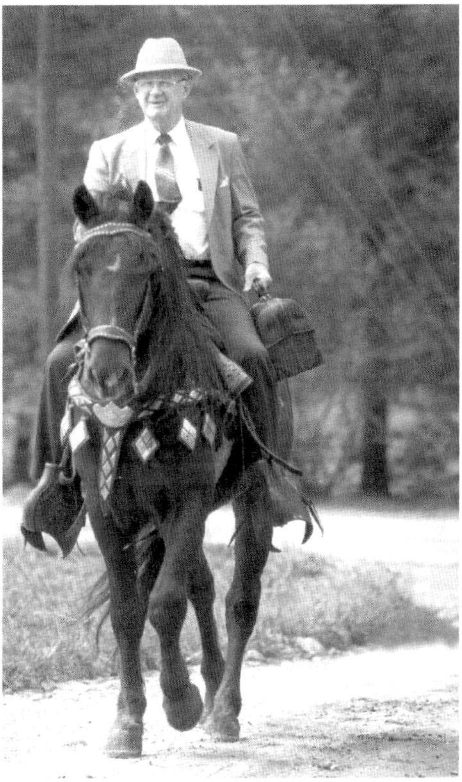

Dr. Joseph Bailey on his way to make a house call, circa 1960s. *Photo courtesy of Joseph Bailey Jr.*

He arrived with his shirt open down the front, and a gaping hole had been cut in his undershirt to afford full ventilation of his malady. Patients who had come in ahead of him and had the right to be seen first seemed to realize it would be unwise to subject themselves to a prolonged view of his particular ailment, so no one complained when he was promptly taken into the treatment room.

An Old Friend at Christmastime

Christmas is a time of remembering and a time when I'll be thinking especially of a friend who lived alone on her mountainside after her brother and sister passed on. It had been the place of her birth soon after the Civil War was over, and she had never had any desire or reason to live elsewhere. Each day of her life was filled with the hardships of pioneer ways, but contentment, not weariness, softened her weathered face until the end of her ninety-four years.

On Saturdays, she walked into town carrying a large basket filled with eggs and home-churned butter, freshly dressed fryers and jams or jellies made from whatever fruit or berry was in season. The open road would have been easier to walk, but she knew shortcuts across her mountain, reducing the miles to seven each way instead of ten, and she didn't mind at all the hills that had to be climbed. She could have ridden in the wagon with her brother, but she said the jolting hurt her back, and walking came easier to her.

When Christmastime was drawing close, though, she rode, for she had more to carry than her basket could hold. She had holly branches and galax leaves and yards of bright green turkey foot that she would mail to her friends in Charleston who counted on her to send such decorations from the mountain they always climbed as soon as they were settled in their summer colony of Flat Rock.

As a child, she lived too far from the one-room schoolhouse at the foot of her mountain for a little girl to walk down the long road and back up when school let out each afternoon, so she never learned to read and write. But when she was ready to send her Christmas bundle of holly and turkey foot and galax to Charleston, she walked a mile down her mountain to ask her niece to "back" the bundle, meaning to address it, the term resulting from the custom of placing an address on what was considered the back of an envelope or package.

Since my friend's mailbox stood at the far end of her road and close to a mile from her house, she allowed ample time to pass before she walked back down to see if a letter had come, letting her know her gift had arrived. If she found the letter, she went on to have her niece read it to her.

Although my friend was often in town to trade butter and eggs for necessities such as coffee and sugar, she never knew the simplicity of dropping into a store to buy a gift. Nor could she have afforded it. Yet she had saved some money. She wrapped it in brown paper and tucked it at the far end of a beam that crossed the ceiling of her house. An attorney persuaded her to put the money in a bank box, which she finally did, signing her transaction with an X to represent her signature.

The time came when she needed her money. She was instructed to make her X, but she refused. Insisting the money belonged to no one but her, she saw the request as an affront to her honesty that had no cause to be questioned. Finally, in order to get the business attended to, the person who had taken her to the attorney's office served as her proxy and left her integrity unscathed.

I'll be thinking of my old friend especially at Christmastime, and my memories of a true mountain woman will be happy ones.

Afterword

Ironically, Louise Howe Bailey also was ninety-four when she left her earthly existence two days after Christmas 2009. In the company of her son, Joe, and his wife, Susan; granddaughters Bevin and Beth; Beth's husband, Edmundo Quiñones; and Susan's family of Clarkes, Louise spent a delightful Christmas at her beloved home, Laurelhurst. I was honored to

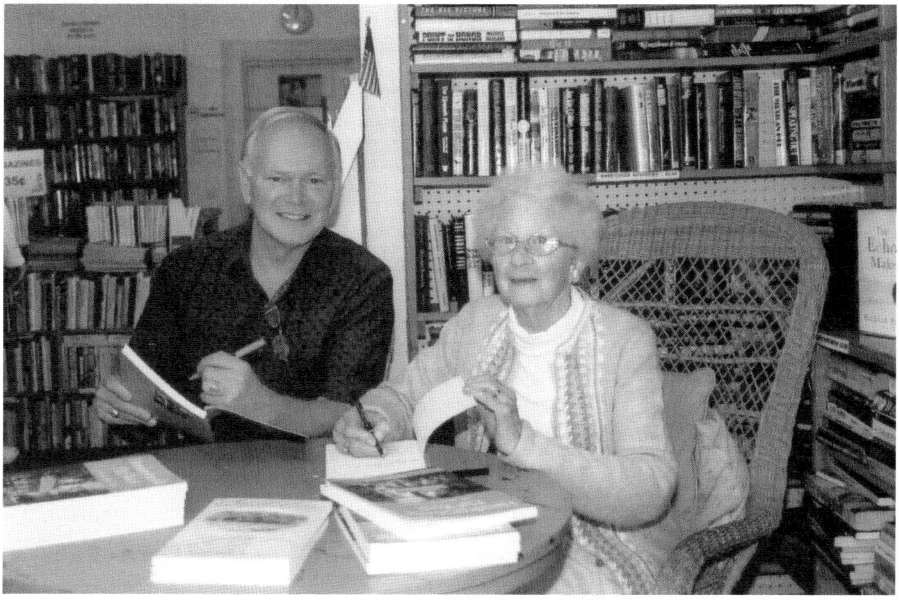

Louise Bailey and Terry Ruscin signing copies of their books at Flat Rock's Book Exchange, 2007. *Photo by Ivy Cowell.*

be a part of the gathering, to share some laughs and holiday fare and to hold Louise's hand, listening to stories recalled in her delightful, soothing voice.

Louise Howe Bailey lived life to its fullest right up to its conclusion. For that we are pleased, yet we sorely miss her presence among us.

—Terry Ruscin

Index

T

V

W

About the Author and Compilers

Louise Howe Bailey was an award-winning local author, storyteller and historian and lifelong resident of Henderson County. For forty-two years, she wrote the column "Along the Ridges" for the *Hendersonville Times-News*. In the second half of her life, Bailey also authored nine books, gave nearly five hundred talks on local history and heritage and led countless tours of her home church, St. John in the Wilderness in Flat Rock. Bailey's awards include the Western North Carolina Historian of the Year Award, the North Carolina Society of Historians Religious Book Award and the Order of the Longleaf Pine—the highest honor bestowed by the State of North Carolina. Henderson County municipalities and the Polk County town of Saluda proclaimed "Louise Bailey Day" on September 25, 2009.

Terry P. Ruscin, an author, photographer, historian and retired advertising executive is a member of the Henderson County Genealogical and Historical Society, Inc., and Historic Flat Rock, Inc. He is also a member of Hendersonville's DRAC (Design Review Advisory Committee) overseeing the city's historic districts, the Henderson County Historic Resources Commission and a former board member of the Henderson County Heritage Museum and the California Missions Foundation. Recently filmed as part of a documentary tribute (DVD) to Louise Howe Bailey's life and influence on Henderson County, Ruscin is also a close personal friend of the Bailey family. He is editor of the international newsletter *¡Siempre Adelante!* and wrote the books *Hendersonville & Flat Rock: An Intimate Tour*; *Dining & Whining*; *Los Duendes*; *Taste for Travel*; and *Mission Memoirs* and was a collaborator on *An Uncommon Mission* and *Santa Margarita Asistencia*.

Joseph P. Bailey Jr. helped Terry compile the articles and images for this volume of Louise Bailey's work. Joe was born in Hendersonville, North Carolina, in 1948, the eldest of Joseph Sr. and Louise Howe Bailey's three sons. After graduating from Hendersonville High School, Joe served four years in the U.S. Navy. He then earned a bachelor's degree from the University of North Carolina at Asheville and a master's degree in biology from Appalachian State University. He was a career teacher in the Henderson County Public Schools and has taught as an adjunct faculty member at several of the nearby colleges. Joe is an avid outdoorsman and is blessed with the Howe-Bailey sense of humor. He lives in Flat Rock and is married to Susan Anne Clarke, also a Henderson County native. Joe and Susan have two daughters, Bevin and Elizabeth.